C0-AOF-510

CONCILIUM

concilium 1998/3

WOMEN'S SACRED SCRIPTURES

Edited by

Kwok Pui-Lan and
Elisabeth Schüssler Fiorenza

SCM Press · London
Orbis Books · Maryknoll

BL
625.7
.W67
1998

Published by SCM Press Ltd, 9–17 St Albans Place, London N1
and by Orbis Books, Maryknoll, NY 10545

Copyright © Stichting Concilium

English translations © 1998 SCM Press Ltd and Orbis Books, Maryknoll

All rights reserved. No part of this publication may be reproduced, stored in a
retrieval system, or transmitted, in any form or by any means,
electronic, mechanical, photocopying or otherwise,
without the prior written permission of
Stichting Concilium, Prins Bernhardstraat 2 6521 A B Nijmegen, The Netherlands

ISBN: 0 334 03049 8 (UK)
ISBN: 1 57075 189 7 (USA)

Typeset at The Spartan Press Ltd, Lymington, Hants
Printed by Biddles Ltd, Guildford and King's Lynn

Concilium Published February, April, June, October, December.

Contents

Introduction

Elisabeth Schüssler Fiorenza

This feminist theology issue of *Concilium* sets out to explore in the *first part* wo/men's[1] experiences in transgressing scriptural boundaries and authority claims and their problematic relations with hegemonic canons and scriptures. In the *second part* it explores the words and practices of wo/men as sacred and reclaims the power of women's memories, words, traditions and texts as enduring heritage and sustaining bread in the struggles for liberation and transformation. However, this volume does not intend to be just another collection of essays on feminist biblical hermeneutics. Rather, it seeks to broaden the discussion theoretically in such a way that critical feminist work on the malestream scriptural canons of the diverse religions of the world as well as the feminist reclaiming of wo/men's sacred power of naming can come into view.

From its inception Christian feminist theology has wrestled with biblical authority and interpretation. Whereas some feminists have rejected the Bible as totally patriarchal, others have insisted that the Bible is a resource in the struggle for liberation. The present volume, however, is deliberately not designated as a project of *biblical* hermeneutics since this would limit its scope and perspective to the canon of biblical religions. Rather, we have chosen the title *Women's Sacred Scriptures* in order to signify a more comprehensive and interactive approach to sacred texts. Hence, the volume seeks to explore writings and traditions which wo/men in the past and in the present have authorized or rejected as their own 'holy scriptures'. It seeks to explore how scriptures become sacred for wo/men and how wo/men's words become scripture for other wo/men.

A critical feminist approach to sacred scriptures, the contributors argue, cannot remain within the boundaries of the written text or of the canon. Rather, it must transgress the textual canonical paradigm because the historical selection of some writings as canonical and the exclusion of others has co-opted, silenced or marginalized those voices and visions that were not acceptable to the dominant group which became identified as 'orthodox'. Thereby the canonization of texts has denied women the sacred authority of the word. A multi-voiced feminist hermeneutics cannot accept the exclusivist religious boundaries that are set either by the process of canonization or by the exclusion of women from theology and scriptural interpretation. Consequently, a critical feminist theology of liberation has to be canonically transgressive and therefore eschew a *biblical* self-limitation.

The term Bible/biblical generally connotes the Protestant notion of revealed texts that serve as the primary locus of authoritative teaching. In order to avoid such Western authoritarian understandings, a comparative religions perspective has sought to develop the notion of scripture as a relational/contextual category. Such a contextual conceptualization of sacred writings that is not derived from Western understandings of the Bible but from the function of sacred texts in historical religions refers to the kinds of religious experiences and the dynamics of relationships that wo/men have had with specially sanctioned texts.

Miriam Levering circumscribes 'scriptures' as 'a special class of true and powerful words, a class formed by the ways in which these particular words are received by persons and communities in their common life'.[2] Such a generic understanding of scriptures problematizes the Western notion of scripture as a single form that offers a sacred story or moral instruction in favour of paying attention to the relations between people and their texts. It challenges the assumption that scriptures are fixed and bounded in canons. It underlines the porousness and unsettledness of scriptural boundaries and brings to consciousness that again and again new scriptural or semi-scriptural forms are created.

Moreover, feminist interpretation cannot conceptualize its project as a *biblical* project, because the Bible has served not only as a means to keep wo/men in their subordinate status but also as a tool of colonization and dehumanization. Because its ethos is inclusive, ecumenical and multicultural, a critical feminist theology of liberation cannot limit itself to biblical canonical writings, accept the authority claims of androcentric scriptures and traditions, or exclusively focus on the teachings of the Bible. Rather it places in the centre of attention wo/men's authority, agency and spiritual needs. It insists that 'revelation' is given for the sake of the salvation of all wo/men without exception. Hence, as I have pointed out in *Searching the Scriptures*,[3] a transgressive feminist scriptural inquiry must adopt a doubled critical approach: it must search the scriptures as one would search the scene of a crime, and it must search them for the 'sacred coin' of lost liberating traditions and their never realized possibilities.

Emphasizing the relations between scriptures and people rather than the authority and normativity of canon underscores that scriptures are to be seen as contingent historical manifestations which must be reinterpreted in ever new situations. Such an approach can pay attention to the various modes of reception and the different ways of scripturalizing that determine the power of such specially sanctioned texts. Moreover, by replacing *Bible* with *scriptures* the volume also seeks to express the ambivalent relationship that marginalized people have to the Bible. It is not only conscious that the process of canonization has selected those texts that were acceptable to the hegemonic communities and leadership in biblical religions. It also considers that canonical authority is gendered, or better kyriarchalized,[4] in so far as it has been established in and through the silencing and exclusion of writings by wo/men and other marginalized people. Consequently, a critical feminist hermeneutics does not privilege the written word but seeks to value wo/men's traditions which are often for the most part oral.

In short, this issue of *Concilium* seeks not only to explore women's problematic relations with hegemonic canons but also to claim the power of 'the Word' as the heritage of the dispossessed in the struggles for liberation and transformation. Feminist theologians have called not only for a critical interpretation of scriptures but also for an affirmation of women's authority and agency in naming new sacred texts. This authority and agency is multi-vocal and multi-focal.

Feminist theologians of all ethnic and religious colours have not only sought to develop new methods of interpretation but also searched for new scriptures. Womanist scholars have reclaimed black wo/men's writings as sacred, whereas mujerista theologians have declared wo/men's lives as 'sacred texts' and Asian wo/men theologians have contextualized the Bible with the sacred scriptures of the great Asian religions. African and indigenous wo/men stress the importance of the oral transmission of their sacred traditions. Others have sought to create a 'Third Testament' by collecting contemporary wo/men's revelatory stories, have called for the inclusion of the scriptures of all wo/men of the world and not just of Western wo/men, and problematized the tensions between Jewish, Muslim and Christian biblical understandings. Most importantly, feminist theologians of diverse theoretical and religious persuasions have recognized that their understanding of sacred scriptures depends not only on their religious convictions but also on their religious 'denominational' locations.

At the end, I want to thank Professor Kwok Pui-lan in the name of the board of *Concilium* for being willing to serve as a guest editor for this volume. I especially appreciate the donation of her valuable time and intellectual energy to this project. Without her critical ideas and energetic work this volume would not have come into existence.

We hope that this volume will initiate a rich inter-religious feminist dialogue on sacred scriptures that has barely begun, although we are very conscious that this is only a beginning. Some of the articles we had envisioned did not materialize; others were not written because we could not find an author who would take on the task. However, we believe that this volume is a good beginning and step in the right directon testifying to wo/men's critical, multivocal and multifocal relations with sacred scriptures, be they written or oral.

Notes

1. I write wo/men in such a fashion both in order to indicate the problematic character of the signifier 'woman' and to use the term as inclusive of men. In so-called inclusive androcentric/kyriocentric language systems wo/men always have to 'think twice' as to whether we are meant. This mode of writing invites male readers to learn how to 'think twice' and to adjudicate whether they are addressed.

2. Miriam Levering, 'Introduction', in M. Levering (ed.), *Rethinking Scripture. Essays from a Comparative Perspective*, Albany, NY 1989, 2.

3. Elisabeth Schüssler Fiorenza (ed.), *Searching the Scriptures* (2 vols), New York and London 1993/1994.

4. I have coined the neologism *kyriarchy* [derived from Greek: the rule of the *kyrios*, i.e. the Lord/Master/Father/Husband; in German *Herrschaft*] in order to communicate that texts and traditions are not just androcentric but kyriocentric, that is, articulated in the interest of elite white Western educated men. Gender as a tool of domination is always infected by race, class, culture, age and colonialism.

I · Women's Experience with Sacred Scriptures

What Scriptures are Sacred Authority? Ambiguities of the Bible in the Lives of Latin American Women

Ivone Gebara

Introduction

The old questions still formulated by students of sacred scripture seem to frighten those to whom they are addressed and who try to answer them. I found this reaction of fright when, researching for this article, I asked several Christian women about the influence and authority of the Bible in their lives. The question seemed surprising and unexpected. It was as though I was forcing them to think about something that did not impinge on their daily concerns. My question seemed to come out of a chest of old junk laid aside as having no useful purpose. But after their initial discomfort they considered the question further, and it provoked reflections beyond its immediate scope.

The first thing that frightened some women of the popular classes was the fact that my question associated the Bible with the notion of authority. I asked if the Bible had authority in their lives. But, for them, linking the Bible and authority seemed rather strange. For many of them, authority is something that belongs to an outside power exercised over their lives, to a coercive force and even to police authority. The Bible seemed different and rather apart from such experiences. Most of the Roman Catholic women I spoke to had little knowledge of the Bible.[1] The little they knew came from the texts they heard at Sunday masses, and even these were heard as disjointed stories, confused one with another. In reality, they had no knowledge properly so-called of the Bible and, as one of them said to me, 'If I don't know something, that thing can't have any real authority in my life.'

In another conversation with another group which had had more religious education, some women remembered the traditional answers they had learned in their youth, answers that referred to scripture as 'The Word of God' with absolute authority over us. Others in the same group remained hesitant and could not make up their minds on the question. They tried to respond according to the new framework of feminism they had adopted, but they could not clearly define their present relationship to the Bible. Yet others called themselves Christians, but with no habit of reading the Bible or looking to it as having authority in their lives. Others again, generally from Protestant churches, stressed the importance of the Bible in providing answers to their questions about the meaning of life. I was struck by the fact that some, particularly from the Pentecostal churches, insisted on the fact that the Bible told them about life after death, and that this was important for knowing how to act in the present life.

Of the women I spoke to, only two had done CEBI (Ecumenical Centre for Biblical Studies) courses, which have undoubtedly helped many women in Latin America to reflect on their lives and their engagement in society and politics. If I had spoken only to them, the results of my survey would probably have been at least partly different. But I chose to talk to the sort of women who, in my view, represented the majority. They made me think of aspects beyond the Bible that other women more closely tied to church structures would probably not have made me do. The result is that this article is limited in scope and expresses points of view that are limited but, in my opinion, interesting to reflect on, above all if one wishes to discover important aspects of the lives of the majority of women.

The varied conversations I had with different groups generally led to an interesting discussion on what authority was and who exercised authority in people's lives. The women I spoke to came from differing social classes, ranging from women who had some leadership role in the poorest *barrios* to university graduates with a good religious formation. What I share in this article is a mixture of experiences, of different discourses, mixed in with my own personal reflections. These discourses nourished me, and it is from them that I received the inspiration and the ingredients out of which I have been able to make and offer this shared 'bread'. I hope it will be tasty and help to feed our hunger for knowledge, for justice and tenderness.

I. What is the source of authority?

Is it the case that the Bible holds the same authority for women? And if it does, what sort of authority is this?

In my conversations I discovered that for most women there is a distinction between accepted authority and imposed authority. There was an equally assertive affirmation of the personal 'I' as authority. The distinctions were not very precise or delineated, but they suggested vital experiences rich in significance. I shall try to give an idea of the ideas put forward and to reflect on their content.

(a) Accepted authority

Accepted authority seems to be that based on reciprocity of relationships. In this sense, a person shares in the 'creation' of this type of authority. It is an authority that comes about because I allow it to exist for me. And it exists for me because in a sense I exist for it. This type of authority can have interpersonal and collective dimensions marked by a shared responsibility. So some women spoke of the authority of friendship or the authority of affective and loving relationships. In such relationships the word of the other is valued and should be respected because it comes from a life that is important for us. Authority 'grows up' or comes into being on the basis of an appreciative assessment, of the 'good will' built into the relationship. The other person becomes an authority because in a way I consent to this. There is a commitment or a complicity that grows in the relationship.

Accepted authority is equally marked by reciprocity, particularly in the form of decisions taken jointly, in the exchange of information or in affective exchange. It is an authority based on responsibility taken on together. Despite the difficulties inherent in all types of human relationship, this sort of authority seems to approximate most closely to the daily experience of most women, or at least to their dreams of how to lead their family and working lives.

As part of this same experience, I also saw how certain types of music, certain paintings and certain books have authority over us. They make such an impression on us that we feel it in our bellies and in our hearts. We maintain, over some time, a relationship of affective authority with them. And when authority is affective it becomes capable of nourishing good relationships, of bringing out certain types of behaviour and even of pushing our bodies into carrying out certain actions. A mobilizing complicity is established. It is as if a work of art, in its different expressions, is awakening hidden feelings, dormant desires, dreams or hopes in us. It is as though it is guiding our lives in certain directions, teaching us something, strengthening our steps, and becoming at times the echo of our own voice, the expression of important aspects of our life. The work seems to express what we want to express. In a way it either takes the place of our words or makes them clear. Through it we can say that 'this' is what we feel or experience.

'Accepted authority' does not always produce right and good deeds of solidarity. For a start, authority cannot be limited to a moralistic type of analysis. One has to describe it, capture its modalities, the beauty and the contradictions it brings into our lives. The main thing is to consider the relationship established between the work and those who admire it and accept it. This relationship is full of ambiguities, paradoxes and riches. It is marked by acceptance of what is 'different' in us, but also by 'likeness', by what confirms the steps we take in life and helps us to move forward.

Often, as we know, the difference that attracts us has a special authority over us. This means that we allow ourselves to be attracted by the feelings or ideas it provokes, without putting up any resistance. So we say that we are 'impassioned' by this person, this book or this picture. And this passion is deeply motivating.

A common attitude to what is 'different', particularly to what seems extremely beautiful and even 'on a higher plane', is to admire it and at the same time affirm it in its relationship to us. This affirmation in relation to us often takes the form of exalting the greatness of the other while at the same time exaggerating the littleness of the admirer. It is similar to the admiration of a pupil for a master, or a poet for the music that inspires him or her. Greatness and littleness seem to exercise a mutual attraction and legitimation. The littleness of one legitimizes the greatness of the other, or vice-versa. In the same way the beauty of one seems to underline the ugliness of another or to show up the vices of others.

Many works of art of great beauty express the violence and ugliness of certain situations. The beauty of expression of human tragedy can thus denounce injustice. So the expression of injustice can become a work of art when it is shown through the inspiration of an artist expressing it with mastery. This ethical-aesthetic reading at first glance seems to enshrine a large dose of dualism and a fair dose of hierarchical conception of human relationships in the extent to which it emphasizes opposites. But at a second glance it shows the mixture and ambiguity present in human existence, and it is of capital importance to realize this.

I see this ambiguity being experienced by some groups of women in their relationship with the personages and diverse situations portrayed in the sacred scriptures. Idealization of past history or of the lives of certain people serves on the one hand as a form of oppression for certain individuals and groups, but on the other hand can also serve as a 'pretext' for liberation. It all depends on the personal and contextual story of those who approach the text. As one woman very interested in the Bible said to me, 'In it I recognize myself as sometimes strong and sometimes oppressed.' There are no absolute laws to define the influence a work will have on those who appreciate it. There is rather a plurivalence depending on the diversity of situations and the relationship of different groups to a text, a work of art or a person.

Another common attitude to what is different, to the 'thing' that challenges us, is to dialogue with it. Ultimately, the text or work of art – and I include film, photography and television here – is a pretext for a dialogue. Such dialogue takes a particular form: the other, the work, is important, but the most important role is that of the subjects who open themselves to this encounter. It is basically always in relation to their own lives that they contemplate and analyse what they see or read. The role of subjectivity denounces the pretension to objectivity of the sciences and their authority. It is as though the scales of the dialogue were weighted more heavily on one side than the other. Interpretation lays greater stress on the lives of the interpreters, of those who provoke the dialogue and seek ways forward from it. It is as though the interpreters take their own lives as their criterion of interpretation. In this sense it could, for example, be said that those who read the Bible have authority over it. 'Accepted authority' sets out to be critical of authoritarian and dominating systems based on a concept of authority 'over people'. And the Bible is included in this category.

(b) Imposed authority

Imposed authority is authority that is not chosen affectively. It is the authority that regulates social relationships. It is authority over people; it exercises a coercive power and has to be accepted in group living and even by some persons in their interpersonal relationships.

In this sense, having authority means developing a power relationship with different qualifications and shades. Imposed authority shows the snares of power that becomes authority over others. On the basis of their experience women denounce various aspects of the labyrinths of power, because these impinge on their lives.

– There are those who usurp power and impose their authority on others.

– There are those who, for a variety of different motives, deliver their lives into the hands of others and relate to them in submissive or authoritarian ways. It is as though they needed a law deriving from 'the other' in order to exist. It is as though autonomy weighs on them and becomes an insupportable burden.

– There are those who call authority 'service' to the highest ideals of humanity and seek legitimation for its exercise in the Bible. In this sense, various groups of women are denouncing the traps set by this 'service-power', especially when it is legitimized by a religious ideology that seeks the purest form of this power in the Bible. Patriarchal religious power often presents itself as 'service-power' and so masks the limitations it subtly introduces into women's lives. For this reason, it needs to be analysed on the basis of the real effects of its actions on people's lives.

From all this, one can deduce that the Bible appears neither as accepted nor as imposed authority in the lives of most women 'of the people'. But it is turned into authority by the strength of those who use it with authority. Its authority stems directly from those who interpret it according to their needs, their religious upbringing or their ideology. It is 'pretext' text, 'instrument', past history continually reactivated to deal with present needs.

In this respect, my perception does not agree with that of Pablo Richard, who seems to insist on the fact that communal reading of the Bible in Latin America takes on the 'cultural, generic and ecological dimension of the People of God'. Furthermore, he states, the interpretation made by the base communities is carried out 'in the tradition of the churches and under the leadership of the church authorities'.[2] This statement does not correspond either to my experience or to that of many colleagues. Are we not still under the same hierarchical system of ideological control? And how do women fit into his scheme? By placing their autonomy in relation to a patriarchal tradition that has marginalized and oppressed them. Richard alludes, at the end of his article, to 'women's viewpoint in interpreting the Bible' but without drawing any consequences related to the novelty introduced by feminist hermeneutics.

(c) The personal 'I' as authority

Reflecting on authority has led some women to discover the source of authority over their lives in themselves. If on the one hand we have to remember the relational and fragile character of our existence, on the other we need to stress the importance of these discoveries as a step towards affirming the autonomy of women. The question 'Who is authority for you?' was most often answered, after some hestiation, with, 'In the first place, I myself'.

I have to admit to being impressed by the force and relevance of such an answer, particularly in the mouths of some women. It was as though they were stating the obvious, something that was part of their everyday lives. Their statement derived its assertiveness from the fact that most of them were undertaking the task of bringing up children and providing for the household virtually on their own. The question was asked of women over forty years of age and burdened by a life marked by a great deal of suffering and struggle. It was as though their daily encounters with a variety of situations had allowed their 'I' to emerge as their authority for themselves. Some who were more familiar with the scriptures illustrated their personal authority with some texts from the Bible, as if the memory of what they had heard confirmed their experiences. Remembrance of the past, of stories listened to, of some verses from the Psalms and phrases from the Gospels, illustrated their account and gave some legitimacy to their interpretation.

For example, one woman speaking of the difficulties of bringing up children, said, 'Isn't it true, though, as the Bible says, that all people do is made up of darnel and wheat?' Another said, after telling of a dispute some women had had with their parish priest, 'This story of women not being allowed to speak in church is already in the Bible. Just shows how long injustice against women has been going.' And finally, another, after describing the difficulty of improving the lot of the poor, concluded, 'I reckon this story of a new heaven and a new earth is not going to come true very soon.'

I call such a use of the Bible informal. In that sense, the authority of the Bible, when it is used, is illustrative or rather serves to give examples, to strengthen positions, to remember an old wisdom. Bits of history, proverbs and sayings are woven into the thread of present history. There is no formal reference or detailed knowledge of the books of the Bible or of the actual life-stories of the people in it. In the end, the Bible is not directly linked to the field of women's essentials, particularly of those who struggle to survive. In the same way, the Bible is not criticized, nor is it spoken of as a patriarchal book. Quite simply, daily life does not lead women to look to the Bible for ways out of the problems they face every day.

More precisely, their informal references to the Bible are interlaced with other references: pieces of popular music, characters from a soap opera on TV whom everyone watches and feels for, events in the neighbourhood used as examples of what is just or unjust. I remember one woman advising another by telling her not to behave 'like the Maria in the seven-o'clock soap'. The most frequent references, however, are to the advice mothers gave their children and grandmothers their grandchildren, with the mother as the dominant figure. One woman told me, 'This business of dealing with people I learned from my mother'; and another said, 'I season meat like my grandmother taught me'. This source of authority seems to be growing as a sort of 'new culture' and new ethic advised by women.

II. The illusion of religious power

While on the one hand I stress the existence of a new sense of power and authority in these groups of women, on the other I should like to underline the illusions that religious power still seems to cling to today. I am more and more convinced that those who hold institutional religious power often refer to an imaginary idea of 'the people', to the people as they would like these to be. And this idea is sometimes of a people submissive to the teachings of the Bible and sometimes of a people still far from the spirit of the gospel. Those who exercise some form of power in the churches would then be responsible for evangelizing or converting them. Furthermore, they see themselves as invested with the power to guide the people along the road to goodness as though they were 'defenceless sheep' in need of shepherds.

Liberation theology has led some intellectuals in the various churches to speak of the Bible as a basic reference for the daily lives of the poor, as an instrument in the struggle for liberation or a light that illuminates the history of the poor. While in fact the biblical movement has been significant in nearly all the countries of Latin America, we need to qualify this statement with the questions: Which Bible has been and is a light to the poor? And who are these poor?

(a) Feminist hermeneutics as politics

Today, with the growth of various facets of the feminist movement, we need to ask how this light (the Bible) illuminates the lives of these poor when they are women. I believe the hermeneutics of liberation theology has failed to pay sufficient attention to the state of oppression in which women find themselves and has not seen the significance of gender in understanding unjust relationships between men and women. This is where feminist hermeneutics of the Bible can make its contribution. This is above all a political hermeneutics, since it joins the battle over interpretation of the sacred texts with a well-defined objective,

In this respect, I recognize that the work of women biblicists and theologians has virtually no impact on the lives of women who use Christian teaching as a reference point, but it does open a front of conflictual dialogue on the institutional level. This is the point where I situate the political battle, aimed at occupying spaces on the level of interpretation, of construction of meaning, and finally on that of church authority.

Feminist hermeneutics is breaking the mould of masculine hegemony in biblical knowledge by putting forward a different interpretation of the texts and by showing up the ambiguities of masculine power in its own interpretation of the texts. The process of deconstruction and reconstruction carried out by feminism extends the actual meaning of texts and brings out relationships originally hidden from readers formed in the patriarchal tradition. It is gradually having an influence on culture and creating new ways of viewing relationships among people.

For example, feminist hermeneutics denounces the 'power to put to death' that is a continual feature of patriarchal experience of power. In consequence, this power produces a model of being a man, of being a hero, of being dominating and warlike, that has become the highest expression of the sort of virility that most cultures admire.[3] Following this route, women biblicists and theologians point to the structure that sustains the 'kyriarchal system', as Elisabeth Schüssler Fiorenza calls it,[4] and are working on showing the different strands of powers of domination at work beyond those shown by an analysis that considers only class domination. Even if this institutional political dimension of feminist hermeneutics does not touch the daily lives of poor women directly, it is in my view nevertheless completely at their service, since they are the first victims of patriarchal religious domination.

Another aspect – of fundamental importance in my opinion – being denounced by Latin American women biblicists and theologians is the abstract character of universalist masculine discourse on liberation. In masculine theological thinking, hope is often to be found more in discourse on eschatological hope than in the little actions and achievements of every day. Besides this, masculine discourse fears the expression of 'no hope', just as it fears talk of the non-sense of some lives and some deaths. So it develops a theory of martyrdom based on the transformation of barbarity and violence into plausible discourse. Through its discourse on idealized martyrdom it then redeems violent sacrifice as a utopic form of ransoming liberty.

We women of Latin America are prepared to denounce the absolute lack of meaning of violent deaths, of deaths through malnutrition, from lack of health care, occasioned by all types of war. There is no need to transform violence and make it into something useful or better. There is no need to turn suffering into a source of hope. We know beforehand that our conquests of autonomy and respect are stained with sorrow and tears. We do not deny the cross we carry, but we do not want to make it a symbol of our hope. Martyrs are no use to us if we go on repeating structures and actions of violence.

In my view, the way these women think and act is increasingly weakening masculine messianisms, as well as salvation processes that exalt martyrdom or 'laying down one's life' and base this exaltation on the authority of the Bible. We women are perhaps more prepared to accept the fact that there may be no explanation to justify our suffering. Our basic task is to avoid the crosses laid on us and collectively to cure the ills that come upon us in a thousand and one ways. Our deepest desire is to be happy, to live dignified lives enjoyably.

III. The consolation of religion for poor women

Where will our consolation come from? Who will dry our tears? Who will dare to sing songs of hope when so many of our children have died? Who will help us to win the promised land? What ointments will heal our wounds? Who will hold us up when old age makes us incapable of walking on our own? These questions and lamentations go with me whenever I meet groups of poor women. It is as though they understand the consolation of religion ever anew, even in the midst of the contradictions religion itself produces. I should like to share some of my experiences in order to clarify this perception and the questions it raises.

A few weeks ago I was invited to reflect on hope with a group of fifty poor craftswomen. They had been reflecting on free-market policies and their dire effects on the lives of craftswomen. They were being helped by a group of feminist intellectuals from a non-governmental agency. The methodology employed allowed them to make analyses on the basis of their own experience and also to envisage alternative collective economic strategies. Such alternatives were proving difficult for a whole host of reasons. I was listening to all this with a precise purpose: I was to help feed their hopes of better days to come, at the end of the discussion – not an easy task! I had money to buy some of the wonderful embroideries they were producing, I could appreciate the bags and rugs, towels and dolls on display. I did not need to sell my 'discourse' in order to eat, while they needed to sell their art in order to survive. We were looking for hope together, but in different situations.

Even before I could begin my task, some of the women said they felt the lack of 'praying' and 'songs' to enliven the meeting. And immediately, religious chants began, together with invocations and petitions. This was an ecumenical group, sharing a language of suffering and injustice. They could all take part in this talk of tears and sorrows. There was no need for the 'group animators' to guide them into forms of expression. All those taking part had something to say about their quest for hope, their frustrations and setbacks. Almost all the petitions ended by calling on the power of God to help them, and calling the cross of Christ to mind. The prayers said took forms that would have suited any feminist sensibility, if analysed critically. But that was not the time for any analysis, even a feminist one. It was the time of 'beyond words'; the time for lament and prayer without looking for the meaning of the words but simply looking at the faces, listening to the voices, the sobs and the sighs.

The hierarchical and exclusive language of prayer was the only one available in the cultural universe of those women, and they used it also to inveigh against *machismo* and hierarchies. They cried out to God as their hope when they could hardly hope for any improvement in the economic conditions of their own lives. What a strange contradiction, to use the language of oppression to seek freedom, to call down the powers of God when these powers seemed to be mixed in with the powers of their oppressors! But in these women's prayers God was always the innocent one . . . God was as innocent as they were of producing social oppression! God was on their side and showed himself in their daring to continue organizing themselves and struggling.

In another meeting with working-class women in leadership positions, in which we were reflecting on the blame attached to women, I analysed the Adamic myth of the origin of evil (Genesis 3) with them. Little by little I was encouraging them to find another way of reading the text, and together we were discovering the figure of Eve to be considerably more likeable and active than she has been presented in the various churches. We saw the figure of Adam as that of a man without much initiative and pretty fearful and dependent, with more timid and less courageous characteristics than those usually associated with him. Then we spoke of the simplicity of the dialogue between the serpent and the woman and found how interesting this was. We also saw that the image presented of God was in effect rather like that of a king or a powerful lord. From there, it was easy to talk a little about the historical and political context in which the text was written and to see that the images of God given to us correspond to social and political constructs serving the interests of certain groups. The joy and excitement this produced in the group were impressive. It was as though together we had found the 'pearl of great price' or 'lost drachma'. These women seemed to have found better weapons to use in their struggle to win dignity. They dismantled one form of knowledge and erected another, which gave them greater strength and security.

I cannot really say whether or not the Bible was an authority for them. I could only find that biblical texts explained in 'another way' seemed to become allies of liberation and to satisfy their hunger and thirst for justice. Authority in interpretation derived from their own struggle for dignity and respect. Authority in interpretation came from their experience of rejection, of oppression, and from their deep desire to be considered citizens with equal rights. Authority in interpretation came from their thirst for justice and citizenship. The Bible that formerly seemed to oppress them and give them a negative vision of themselves now showed a different face. The weapons of oppression seemed to have turned into forces of liberation.

In my view, it was they who gave new authority to the text. The text had now become rather an ally in their struggles. The text they had learned in their religious upbringing was slowly beginning to stop discriminating against them; the text was being introduced as a reinforcement in their daily struggles. One of these women made me think of the disciples at Emmaus when she said loudly: 'People feel in their hearts that this story of Adam and Eve has not been told properly. Now I need to share this fire that consumes me and this new bread I am eating with you.'

Conclusion

What scriptures are sacred authority? This was my initial question, a question I come back to in this brief conclusion. In this article the question will remain always a question, to call for and put forward ever new answers.

The question of the authority of the sacred texts has throughout seemed ambiguous, paradoxical, varied and beyond a single answer. We have seen that it is impossible to settle on any one interpretation or to generalize from particular situations. The text is mixed with the context, authority with need, the law with desire. Everything seems to be stirred together like a well-seasoned Latin American salad. The sacred, authority, various quests become part of the ingredients and seasonings of life. The same authority can now be either sweet or bitter. It can either be both at the same time or one or the other as time passes. The general rule is the diversity ordered by life.

Such discoveries relativize all attempts at absolutizing that religious powers seem to make through their authority and the legitimation they use it to supply. Our experience is rather like a poem by the black poetess Elisa Lucinda:

> It both frightens and calms me,
> to be the bearer of several souls,
> common echo of a single sound,
> reverberating being,
> mirror, likeness,
> to be a mouth,
> mistress of the word with no master,
> so many masters does it have . . .[5]

So are we both singular and plural, unique in the midst of the crowd and a crowd inside ourselves. So are we authoritative authority, impassioned authority, silent authority, silenced authority. So are we both profane-sacred and sacred-profane and -profaned. So are we living Bible and life without the Bible. So are we . . . so be it.

Translated by Paul Burns

Notes

1. On this see Ada-María Isasi-Diaz, 'The Word of God in Us', in E. Schüssler Fiorenza (ed.), *Searching the Scriptures*, New York and London 1993.

2. Pablo Richard, 'Hermeneutica de la Liberación – teoría para una lectura communitaria de la Biblia', *PASOS* 5/1995, 37–43.

3. See the work of the biblicist Nancy Cardoso, 'Maria vai com as outras', in *CEBI* 114, 1997, in the series *Palabra na Vida*.

4. Elisabeth Schüssler Fiorenza, 'Ties That Bind: Domestic Violence against Women', in *Voices from the Third World*, EATWOT, Vol. 18, no. 1, June 1995, 122–67.

5. Elisa Lucinda, 'O poema do semelhante' (Poem of likeness), in *O Semelhante*, Rio de Janeiro 1996, 13.

From Oral Stories to Written Text

Joanna Dewey

As Elisabth Schüssler Fiorenza has shown, early Christianity began with a 'discipleship of equals' and ended with the subordination of women.[1] One of the major reasons for this shift in the status of women was the transition of Christianity from an oral movement to one dependent on the authority of written texts. Women and other marginalized people were able to participate fully as leaders when the movement was as an oral one relying on oral authority within a predominantly oral culture. But beginning in the mid-second century, some Christian leaders began to rely increasingly on manuscripts and on written authority, and within two or three hundred years after that, Christians came to rely on a fixed written canon, the New Testament. The writings of the canon were composed and selected by those few within the Christian movement who were literate, that is, predominantly by educated, relatively high-status males, not by a cross-section of all early Christians. In the process of writing and authorizing texts, women's voices and women's stories were omitted, marginalized, trivialized, and at times suppressed altogether. The shift in Christianity from oral story-telling to written manuscripts and from oral to written authority resulted in the loss of many women's voices and the distortion and minimalization of the women's traditions that survived into the written text. In this article, I shall first give a brief description of orality and literacy in antiquity and discuss the interaction of orality, textuality and access to power. Then I shall describe two areas in the New Testament where we can witness the loss or suppression of women's voices in the shift from oral to written authority: the Synoptic stories involving women and the Pastoral Epistles.

First-century media world

Technically speaking, the ancient media world was a manuscript culture with high residual orality.[2] But this is to describe the culture from the perspective of the literate elite who indeed used writing to rule the empire. Most people were not literate at all and did not need to be. Estimates of literacy in the Mediterranean basin are as low as two to four per cent of the entire population.[3] In his massive study of the evidence for literacy in antiquity, William Harris suggests a maximum of fifteen per cent of urban males were literate.[4] Literacy rates were lower in villages than in cities and, at all social levels, lower among women than among men. Among the ruling elite (approximately the top two per cent of the population) literacy was the norm among men and common among women. But this group was not represented in the first generations of Christians. In addition, retainers of the elite (the upper military, bureaucracy and property administrators) who carried out much of the actual administration and ruling were also literate. Some household slaves of the elite, both male and female, would function as scribes for their owners.

For the remainder of the population, there was no public education and little if any need for writing. Further, writing materials were awkward or expensive. Potsherds or wax-covered clay tablets gathered in groups of ten, while cheap, were bulky, inconvenient and useless for texts of any length. Parchment and papyrus were used heavily by the elite, but were prohibitively expensive for anyone else. The culture did not support the spread of literacy.

Writing was used to communicate at a distance, to record large financial transactions, and to keep debt records. Long-distance trade needed writing; for example, Lydia, if she was involved in an international luxury trade, would have employed scribes and may have been literate herself. Letters were used to communicate over a distance, as Paul communicated with the churches he founded. Wills, marriages and divorces involving substantial property would be recorded in writing, but that affected only those with wealth. If the poor, some ninety per cent or more of the population, ever needed writing at all, it would be for an apprenticeship agreement or to communicate with relatives living far away and, for this writing or reading, they would hire a scribe. For the huge majority of people, illiteracy was neither an economic nor a social handicap.

For life was basically conducted orally. Official information was broadcast by public criers who were attached to all levels of government. Even more, information and cultural traditions were transmitted by non-literate story-tellers. Four types of story-tellers were common in antiquity: street performers of both sexes who eked out a very marginal existence; a somewhat higher status group who told religious and secular stories outside temples and synagogues, entertaining, teaching and endeavouring to draw people into the particular worship centre; story-tellers of both sexes who did not earn their living at it, but who had local or regional reputations as good story-tellers; and finally, women, mothers or nursemaids, who told stories to educate, amuse or frighten children.[5]

Story-telling was ubiquitous. Oral story-telling would occur in various settings, in the work place, while travelling, to neighbours in the evening, in the household. Much story-telling would take place in gender-segregated groups, but much also would occur in mixed settings. Wherever people gathered, stories were told. Further, stories were not fixed, but continually adapted to and shaped by the particular audience. If someone of relatively high status was present, the story-teller would honour that person; if no such people were present, the story-teller would tell a story in a way that reinforced popular values and popular resentments of the rich. Stories reflected the social locations of their tellers and hearers.

Like everyone else, Christians engaged in story-telling. Individuals would tell stories to other individuals. There were story-tellers who had local or regional reputations. Probably some Christian preachers and teachers were viewed similarly to the story-tellers attached to temples. And like other groups, both women and men told stories. Several early Christian traditions most likely derive from women's story-telling: the stories of the woman with the haemorrhage and the Syrophoenician woman, those of the women connected with the burial and resurrection, and the stories of the women in the apocryphal Acts. Early Christian women were proclaimers and story-tellers as well as receptive listeners.

Oral v. manuscript media: access to authority[6]

Christianity began as a predominantly oral movement. It appealed to oral authorities: to what someone had said or seen or was saying in the Spirit, not to what was written in some text. Oral authority is inherently democratic or egalitarian: the opportunity to gain oral authority is open to most people. Almost everyone is able to speak; good speaking requires skill, practice and experience, but it does not require formal education. Jesus himself is perhaps our prime example of a skilled but not formally educated speaker. Of course, an uneducated illiterate woman could not compete in rhetorical contests against educated men. But she could and apparently did gain authority in local congregations through her speech (I Cor. 14; Rom. 16; Acts 18). Early Christian communities seem to have been made up of mixed but non-elite status people or all quite low-status people. In such groups, the voices of women were heard and some women could gain authority along with some men. The oral medium is a relatively equal-opportunity medium.

Manuscript-based authority, on the other hand, tends to be quite elitist. Literacy is restricted to a few in manuscript cultures. Access to manuscripts and their contents requires formal education and financial resources.

In a patriarchal society such as the Roman Empire, both were concentrated among and largely limited to relatively elite males and their retainers. Most men and almost all women did not have access to such authority. To control the most advanced communications medium of one's day is to hold power in that society. In today's world, those who control access to and the content of television have power over the rest of us. In antiquity, those who controlled access to and the content of writing had power over the rest of society. An analogy that may help to convey the power of writing in antiquity is the power of nuclear weapons today. Few of us know how to make nuclear weapons, even fewer of us control their use. Yet a nation's status is in part dependent on possession of such weapons, and we all are affected by our knowledge of nuclear power. The Roman Empire used not only its armies but also its power over the written word to create the most totalitarian empire the West had known until that time.

Early Christianity began as an oral subculture, with full participation and leadership open to all regardless of status and gender. From the beginning some Christians made use of writing (the composers of Q, Paul), but Christian writings only began to be appealed to as authoritative in the mid-second century. But from then on, the power of the most advanced medium – writing – began to assert itself. Gradually certain manuscripts were considered scripture, and leadership was increasingly restricted to educated males, free men who were heads of households. As long as Christianity remained orally based, women had their own oral traditions, told among themselves, and also made significant contributions to the common tradition known to both men and women. Oral tradition did not end as Christian authority became increasingly manuscript-based. Women continued to tell and hear stories, for they and most men remained non-literate into the modern period.

Two things, however, did change as manuscripts proliferated and became authoritative. First the role of women was minimized and marginalized from what it was in the oral stories, as the stories were written down by the few relatively high-status literate men. Secondly, the content of the oral stories told by women would be determined less and less by their own memories and handing on of traditions, and more and more by what circulated back into oral telling from the manuscripts. The written tradition increasingly controls the content of the continuing oral tradition. These processes have been observed in modern cultures in the transformation of oral traditions to the print medium as will be discussed below.

The shift in Christianity in the second and following centuries to reliance on manuscript authority is not, of course, the only reason for the subordination of women within the church. Other sociological and theological factors, such as the growing institutionalization of the church, the shift from private houses to public buildings, and the increased emphasis on sacrifice, greatly influenced the marginalization of women. But the move to manuscript authority and literate power was important in its own right, and has continued to have an impact on generations into the present, since it is the written texts of the New Testament that still form our imagination about Jesus, the early church and early Christian women.

European folktale and Synoptic stories of women

Alas, we cannot compare the ancient stories told by women with the stories written in our Gospel texts. But we can compare what happened to European folktales as they were written down by educated men.[7] We can compare the earliest printed versions of Charles Perrault (1697) and the Grimm brothers (1812) with oral versions collected again in the early years of this century. The printed versions minimize and trivialize the roles of female characters; the printed versions also gradually supplant and control the oral stories mothers tell their children. The story of Red Riding Hood provides a good example. In Perrault's version, the story ends with the girl being eaten by the wolf. The Grimms' version, partly dependent on Perrault, ends with the girl being rescued by (male) huntsmen. The girl is left dead or needing to be rescued by a male authority figure. In the oral version, the girl also gets herself into trouble with the wolf. However, she extricates herself *by her own initiative* and lives to tell the tale.[8]

Other folktales suffered a similar fate. Alison Lurie shows that the tales we know today are the result of skewed selection and silent revision of what she calls subversive texts.[9] The initial edition of the Grimms' *Children and Household Tales* portrayed sixty-one female characters with magic powers and only twenty-one male characters with magic powers. But each successive edition gave the females less to do and less to say, and omitted altogether stories such as the one of a sleeping prince rescued by an active heroine. And it is these limited printed versions that children learn today.[10] The tendency has been continued into electronic media. Of the three tales from Perrault's and Grimms' collections that Disney filmed (Sleeping Beauty, Snow White, Cinderella), all three have heroines who are 'passive and pretty . . . unusually patient, obedient, industrious, and quiet', and all three have female villains. Yet the tales themselves include many rather feisty female heroines and a plethora of male villains.[11] The control of the most advanced communications medium has been and continues to be used to control the population in general.

The Gospel stories suggest that a similar process of minimizing the role of women has occurred. In the Synoptic tradition, there are ten accounts of miracles involving women and thirty-three accounts involving men. The stories about men are, on the average, two or three verses longer than the stories concerning women – they take up more time in the telling and the listening. Further, the men speak more to Jesus, and Jesus to the men, than the women speak or are spoken to.[12] Thus not only are stories about men included three times as often, but they are given more narrative emphasis.

Besides the miracle stories, there is another group of seven stories, told in thirteen versions, involving minor characters, stories such as the anointing stories, the great commandment, the widow's mite. In this group, four or *more than half* involve women, suggesting that the predominance of miracle stories involving males reflects male bias rather than a preponderance of male miracle stories in the oral tradition. The portrayal of the women in these stories, however, is strange. The women act but they do not speak. Rather, what is portrayed is that Jesus and other men sit around and talk to each other about what the women are doing.[13] A striking example is the narrative picture of a woman weeping over Jesus' feet and drying them with her hair, while the men continue their dinner party and discuss her behaviour with one another, although Luke's Jesus does finally speak to the woman. This scenario is characteristic of these stories – the woman is used as an example to instruct men. I suggest that the preponderance of miracles involving males and the silent role of women in the non-healing narratives is not representative of the oral tradition, but rather reflects a minimizing and distortion of women's roles similar to that which occurred to the folktales as they were put into print by educated men.

The Pastoral Epistles v. the women of the apocryphal Acts

Above, in the discussion of the Synoptic stories of women, I looked at what happened to the oral stories on the model of what happened to oral folktales in Europe as they were put into print. In the following discussion of the Pastoral Epistles, I am discussing an instance of writing being used directly to counter oral stories of women. And while some of those oral stories did survive in writing they did not make it into the New Testament canon, while the Pastoral Epistles attempting to silence women did.

The Pastoral Epistles, I and II Timothy and Titus, contain some of the strongest injunctions against women's leadership. 'Let a woman learn in silence with full submission. I permit no woman to teach or to have authority over a man; she is to keep silent' (I Tim. 2. 11–12). The reader is warned: 'Have nothing to do with profane myths and old wives' tales' (4.7). People to be avoided include 'those who make their way into households and captivate silly women' (II Tim. 3.6). The pastor admonishes, 'tell the older women . . . to teach what is good, so that they may encourage the young women to love their husbands, to love their children, to be self-controlled, chaste, good managers of the household, kind, being submissive to their husbands' (Titus 2.3–5). These texts are part of the New Testament canon; they have been and still are used to control Christian women's behaviour. Read from the pulpit today, they appear as general injunctions valid for all time. Such is the power of an authoritative *written* text.

Yet in their own time of composition the Pastorals were not a description of how actual Christian women were behaving. Rather they were *prescriptive* texts, reflecting the author's ideal of what a church should be like, what the author thinks particular groups should or should not do, how they should behave. As such they provide historical evidence for the existence of Christians who do not believe or act in ways the author approved, for prescriptive statements are evidence that the opposite behaviour is occurring. One does not need to tell women to learn in silence and not take authority over men if indeed women are being silent and submissive. Only when women are actively claiming their own authority are such injunctions given.

Written in the early second century, the Pastorals represent one voice in a debate among Christians about the legacy of Paul. As Dennis MacDonald has shown, these writings oppose the view of Paul and women found in the stories preserved in the apocryphal Acts of Paul.[14] In them, Paul appears as a wandering charismatic preacher and miracle worker in conflict with political authorities, preaching chastity as a universal Christian requirement. Women who hear his preaching abandon their husbands and households to follow Paul in a life of celibacy. Some, such as Thecla, become wandering teachers and miracle workers themselves, and their stories inspired other women to follow their examples.[15] Thecla was a popular saint throughout the early centuries of the church and her story was widely known. The story clearly derives from women's storytelling; we are fortunate that it was written down and survived at all.[16]

The Pastorals appear to be written to oppose such understandings of Christianity, to silence women and re-embed them in the patriarchal household. The writings are pseudonymous; the author thereby attempts to claim the authority of Paul for his view of the proper role of women, countering the view of stories such as Thecla. Quite likely the writings were never sent to particular individuals at all but were composed to be part of a codex of Christian writings.[17] If one had lived in the second to fifth centuries and beyond, one likely would have heard and known the story of Thecla, for it could easily be remembered, be told and retold. One would have heard the Pastorals rarely, only when they were read aloud in church. And even then, they would be heard by people who knew and honoured groups of celibate women, who knew that the view of the Pastorals was not the only way for women to serve God.

The writings included in the canon were not chosen by Christians as a whole. Rather they were selected by bishops who were literate men. Not surprisingly, they included the Pastoral Epistles, which conformed to their ideas of proper household and church order, and rejected the Acts of Thecla. And the written text gradually supplanted the oral stories. In the age of print, when the Bible, and only the Bible, was first put in one volume, the Pastorals survived and stories not in the canon were forgotten altogether, so that most Christians today have never heard of Thecla. The written attempt to silence the women's oral stories is all that we read and know today.

Conclusions

The New Testament is not a value-neutral survey of early Christianity. It is biassed in favour of those of higher social location, primarily educated, literate men who held to a patriarchal ideal including the subordination of women. When they wrote and edited their texts, they told the stories their way. The stories empowering women, told and retold among women and sometimes in mixed groups, did not often make it into the canon and, when they did, they were distorted and trivialized. Prescriptions limiting and controlling women, on the other hand, had no problem being included in the authoritative text. The limited portrayal of women and the injunctions concerning their behaviour continue to limit and deform the lives of Christian women today. We need to remember, however, that the New Testament presents only the tip of the iceberg of the stories of women, and that the stories are skewed.

The writing, however, has also preserved some important women's traditions over time. Had the Gospel writings not been recognized as authoritative soon after their composition, we might have lost even more women's stories and women's history. For in spite of patriarchal editing, there is a considerable amount of material about women in the Gospels and letters. The women have not been written out altogether. For example, the stories of the women discovering the empty tomb were retained when the Gospels were written. But Tatian, writing a conflation of the Gospels in the late second century, trivialized them by turning them into the wives of the Twelve, not independent followers of Jesus. Who knows what more would have been lost if the texts had not become authoritative but had remained open to alterations.

Yet it is important not to absolutize the New Testament. We need to mourn the women's stories that have been lost. We need to remember, reimagine and reinvent what we can, in order to empower ourselves today. We are entitled to the same freedom the ancient literate men took with the stories. Today we should honour and encourage and celebrate women's voices.

Notes

1. E. Schüssler Fiorenza, *In Memory of Her: A Feminist Theological Reconstruction of Christian Origins*, New York and London 1983.

2. W. Ong, *Orality and Literacy: The Technologizing of the Word*, London and New York 1982, 158.

3. B. Malina and R. Rohrbaugh, *Social-Science Commentary on the Synoptic Gospels*, Minneapolis 1992, 3; M. Bar-Ilan, 'Illiteracy in the Land of Israel in the First Centuries CE', in *Essays in the Social Scientific Study of Judaism and Jewish Society*, Hoboken, NJ, 2, 56.

4. William Harris, *Ancient Literacy*, Cambridge, MA and London 1989, 267. The following description of literacy is heavily dependent on Harris. For a fuller description, see J. Dewey, *Textuality in an Oral Culture: A Survey of the Pauline Traditions, Orality and Textuality in Early Christian Literature*, Semeia 65, 39–47.

5. A. Scobie, 'Storytellers, Storytelling, and the Novel in Graeco-Roman Society', *Rhenisches Museum für Philologie*, 122, 229–59.

6. See J. Dewey, 'From Storytelling to Written Text: The Loss of Early Christian Women's Voices', *Bib Theo Bull* 26, 1996, 74–5.

7. Ibid., 75–6.

8. The versions are all found in J. Zipes (ed.), *The Trials and Tribulations of Little Red Riding Hood*, New York and London ²1993. The oral version was collected by P. Delarue.

9. A. Lurie, *Don't Tell the Grown-ups: Subversive Children's Literature*, Boston 1990.

10. Ibid., 16–28. See also Kay Stone, *Things Walt Disney Never Told Us, Women and Folklore*, Austin and London 1975, 42–50.

11. Stone, *Things Walt Disney Never Told Us* (n. 10), 44.

12. J. Dewey, 'Women in the Synoptic Gospels. Seen but not Heard?', *Bib Theol Bull* 1997, 54–7.

13. Ibid., 57–8.

14. D. MacDonald, *The Legend and the Apostle. The Battle for Paul in Story and Canon*, Philadelphia 1983.

15. The text of the Acts of Thecla may be found in W. Schneemelcher and R. McL. Wilson, *New Testament Apocrypha*, Louisville and Cambridge ²1992, 2, 239–46.

16. MacDonald, *The Legend and the Apostle* (n. 14); S. McGinn. 'The Acts of Thecla', in *Searching the Scriptures. A Feminist Commentary*, New York and London 1994, 2, 800–28.

17. D. Aune, *The New Testament in Its Literary Environment*, Philadelphia 1987, 205.

Canonization and Marginalization: Mary of Magdala

Karen L. King

Mary of Magdala is best known in popular Western imagery and tradition as a repentant prostitute,[1] as the adulteress rescued by Jesus from men trying to stone her,[2] and as the woman sinner whose tears of repentance washed Jesus' feet in preparation for his burial.[3] Yet none of this is historically accurate. Nothing in the New Testament or early Christian literature provides a shred of evidence to support this portrait.

Historically Mary was a Jewish woman who followed Jesus of Nazareth. She came from the town of Magdala, located on the west shore of the Sea of Galilee, just north of the city of Tiberias. Apparently of independent means, she accompanied him during his ministry and supported him out of her own resources.[4] The New Testament Gospels[5] and other early Christian literature consistently portray Mary as a prominent disciple of Jesus.[6]

In the Gospel stories, she is said to have been present at the crucifixion[7] and to have been a witness to the resurrection.[8] Indeed, she is portrayed as the first or among the first privileged to see and speak with the risen Lord.[9] In the Gospel of John, the risen Jesus gives her special teaching and commissions her as an apostle to the apostles to bring them the good news.[10] The Gospel of Mary, an early second-century text discovered at the end of the nineteenth century in Egypt, also affirms that Mary received special teaching from Jesus and functioned as a leader among the disciples after the resurrection. The combined evidence strongly suggests that Mary was a visionary and leader in the Christian movement after Jesus' death.

How are we to understand and account for these different portraits, for the simultaneous *canonization* of Mary as a prominent disciple and her *marginalization* as a repentant prostitute?

The simplest answer is that the problem arose due to misguided exegesis. Starting in the fourth century, Christian theologians in the Latin

West began confusing Mary of Magdala with Mary of Bethany.[11] They conflated the account of John 12.1–8, in which Mary of Bethany anoints Jesus in preparation for his burial, with the account of the unnamed sinner woman in Luke 7.36–50 who washed Jesus' feet with her tears and anointed them. From there it was an easy step to identify Mary of Magdala with the unnamed adulteress in John 8.1–11. Mary the disciple had become Mary the whore. We can perhaps see this confusion as simply an error – there are after all a lot of Marys to keep straight: Mary of Magdala, Mary of Bethany, Mary the mother of Jesus, Mary the wife of Clopas (Jesus' aunt), Mary the mother of James the younger and Joses (or Joseph), and of course the 'other' Mary. But the simplicity of this answer is deceptive. The Eastern Orthodox churches after all never made this mistake. Even in the West, the connections were not made until relatively late. The church fathers of the early centuries knew nothing of Mary as a prostitute; they mentioned her primarily as an important witness to the resurrection. They are concerned, of course, to counter any hint that Jesus' command to Mary not to touch him (John 20.17) might imply that the resurrection was not physical, but no criticism is directed at Mary. Indeed Tertullian praised Mary because she approached Jesus to touch him 'out of love, not from curiosity, nor with Thomas' incredulity'.[12] The reason for the prohibition was simply that it was too early for touching; the resurrection had to be completed by Jesus' ascent.[13]

By the sixth century, however, another interpretation had become prevalent, exemplified in a sermon by Pope Gregory the Great in which he not only identified Mary of Magdala with the sinner women of Luke and John, but also drew the moral conclusion that would dominate the imagination of the West:

> She whom Luke calls the sinful woman, whom John calls Mary, we believe to be the Mary from whom seven devils were ejected according to Mark. And what did these seven devils signify, if not all the vices? . . . It is clear, brothers, that the woman previously used the unguent to perfume her flesh in forbidden acts. What she therefore displayed more scandalously, she was now offering to God in a more praiseworthy manner. She had coveted with earthly eyes, but now through penitence these are consumed with tears. She displayed her hair to set off her face, but now her hair dries her tears. She had spoken proud things with her mouth, but in kissing the Lord's feet, she now planted her mouth on the Redeemer's feet. For every delight, therefore, she had had in herself, she now immolated herself. She turned the mass of her crimes to virtues, in order to serve God entirely in penance, for as much as she had wrongly held God in contempt.[14]

Mary lost all semblance of the devoted disciple and visionary. She became a model for women to immolate themselves for their crimes of sexuality, vanity and bold speech. Simple error is not sufficient to account for this unsavoury and totally fantastic portrait.

Certainly this invention is part and parcel of typical Western patriarchal constructions of gender roles, which all too often define women almost solely according to heterosexual roles in relation to men. As the Christian model of female sexuality redeemed, Mary took her place with two other prominent figures: the temptress Eve and the virgin mother Mary. Among them, they modelled the roles possible for women in the patriarchal script. But why choose Mary for the role of the repentant sinner? The serious effort necessary to contrive and sustain these strained exegetical connections certainly show that it was not a casual exercise. Did they go to all this trouble simply because they wanted to fill the role with a well-known actor?

Let me suggest another possibility. Patriarchal exegetes invented this role for Mary of Magdala because they wanted to discredit the theology associated with her name and to undermine her significance as a model for the legitimacy of women's leadership. In short, the portrait of the repentant sinner was invented to counter an earlier and very powerful portrait of Mary as a visionary prophet, exemplary disciple and apostolic leader.

That such a portrait of Mary existed as early as the second century is shown in a variety of works, most of which were discovered in Egypt within the last century.[15] Though it would be improper to construct a composite portrait of Mary from such varied materials,[16] these sources do agree in giving Mary a role, often a prominent role, among the disciples.[17] For example, in the Dialogue of the Saviour, a second-century dialogue between the Lord and his disciples, Mary responds with particular insight to certain issues. The Lord himself exclaims at her response to a question: 'You make clear the abundance of the revealer!'[18] At another point, the narrator breaks in to explain: 'She uttered this as a woman who had understood completely.'[19] Mary is clearly to be numbered among the disciples who fully comprehended the Lord's teaching.[20] In the canonical Gospel tradition, it is not entirely clear whether women are included among those who are commissioned to go forth and preach the gospel, though the account in Acts clearly indicates that women received the Spirit at Pentecost.[21] In contrast, the Sophia of Jesus Christ, a second-century revelation discourse given by Jesus to his disciples, clearly states that Jesus commissioned women as well as men to preach the gospel. Mary is included by name[22] among those special disciples to whom Jesus entrusted his most elevated teaching, and she takes a role in preaching the gospel.[23] The Gospel of Philip, a second century Valentinian compilation, mentions

Mary as one of the three Marys 'who always walked with the Lord', and she is called his 'companion'.[24] What this designation means becomes clear later in the text when it is stated that the Lord loved her more than all the disciples and he used to kiss her often.[25] Kissing symbolizes the reception of spiritual teaching, as Jesus points out: '[And had] the word gone out from that place it would be nourished from the mouth and it would become perfect. For it is by a kiss that the perfect conceive and give birth. For this reason we also kiss one another. We receive conception from the grace which is in one another.'[26] When the other disciples object to the apparent favouritism Jesus shows Mary, Jesus tells them that they should seek instead to be loved as she is, that is, they should seek the spiritual perfection she has achieved.

The theme of Jesus' special regard for Mary appears with special emphasis in the Gospel of Mary.[27] Here after the Saviour's departure, Mary steps into his place, comforting the grieving disciples and encouraging them and turning their hearts towards a discussion of the Saviour's words. The work also tells of a special revelation which the Saviour had given to Mary in a vision containing advanced teaching about the nature of visionary experience and the journey of the soul after death. At Peter's request, she passes on this teaching to the other disciples. The Gospel of Mary exemplifies Mary's role as apostle to the apostles by portraying her as a prophet, teacher and support for the other disciples.

The Gospel of Mary illustrates Mary's leadership by contrasting her strength of character and spiritual maturity with the fear, ignorance, and jealousy of other disciples. She alone had maintained her composure at the Saviour's departure while the other disciples were weeping and fearing for their lives should they follow the Saviour's command and go out and preach the gospel. In her vision, the Saviour praises her for 'not wavering' at the sight of him. While the other disciples exhibit jealousy and contention over the fact that the Saviour loved her more than them, Mary only demonstrates care toward them, taking up her role of teacher and leader only in response to their need. The Gospel of Mary illustrates the characteristics of spiritual virtue in Mary's calm, in her unwavering faith, her care for the other disciples, her fearlessness in the face of possible persecution, and her advanced spiritual comprehension of Jesus' teachings. In this way, the Gospel of Mary holds up Mary as a model for Christian leadership based on spiritual maturity and prophetic insight. It is because she has achieved spiritual maturity that she is able to teach and care for the others.

Moreover, the Gospel of Mary addresses the topic of women's leadership directly by narrating a story about a controversy among the disciples over Mary's exercise of leadership. In the story, when she finishes teaching the other disciples about her revelation, Andrew and Peter challenge her. Andrew suggests that her teachings are 'strange', but Peter goes further and questions whether the Saviour could really have preferred a woman to them. Their complaints show that they have not really comprehended the Saviour's teaching. Peter's remark is soundly condemned by Levi, who assures Peter that indeed the Saviour did love her more than them, and for good reason. Peter's position is shown up for what it is: an ignorant jealousy which makes it impossible for Peter to see past the distinctions of the flesh to the spiritual insight of Mary's teaching. He is so focussed on his loss of prestige at being instructed by a woman that he fails to learn from her teaching. The Gospel of Mary thus presents the clearest argument for the legitimacy of women's authority and leadership in early Christianity. By insisting that authority should be based on spiritual maturity rather than on sex/gender distinctions,[28] the Gospel of Mary opens up the possibility of an ungendered space in which both women and men could exercise legitimate leadership aimed at teaching, preaching and exercising care for others. It also carefully ties spiritual development to a sharp critique of unjust domination, suggesting an integral connection between the politics of liberation and spirituality.

Controversy between Mary and other male disciples, especially Peter, appears in a number of other works as well,[29] illustrating that Mary was a figure around whom debates were waged over a number of issues, including the importance of visionary experience, the legitimacy of women's leadership, and the meaning of Jesus' teaching. The fact that a Gospel was written in her name and that she appears so prominently in these early writings shows that, like Peter and Paul, she was a figure to whom apostolic appeal was made. Mary of Magdala was therefore a much more important figure in the early church than the canonical portrait of the New Testament allows.

This information should lead us to approach the canonical texts afresh with a hermeneutics of suspicion.[30] For example, in the face of these powerful traditions about Mary, her absence from the Acts of the Apostles[31] takes on a different appearance. Rather than reading the silence in Acts as evidence that Mary was not important to the early church, it is possible to ask if mention of her was omitted on purpose, and to what purpose. It is especially ironic that Mary is not named in the scene where Peter calls for a replacement for Judas to be chosen as 'a witness to the resurrection'. Although the writer of Acts surely understands women to have been present in the group of 120 persons Peter addresses,[32] Peter's speech makes it clear that only men will be considered.[33] Mary's explicit absence from the text is not oversight but strategic to the exclusion of women from positions of apostolic leadership. Because early Christian theology supporting women's leadership was linked with the name of Mary of Magdala, excluding Mary also operated to oppose the theologies[34] circulating in her name.

The Gospel of Mary[35] gives us a good idea of what at least one of those theologies may have looked like.[36] It constructed Christian identity apart from social gender roles, sex and childbearing. It argued that direct access to God was possible for all through the Spirit. Leadership was exercised by those who are more spiritually advanced by giving freely to all without claim to a fixed hierarchical ordering of power. Jesus was understood as a teacher and mediator of wisdom, not as a judge or ruler, and theological reflection centred on the risen Christ, not on suffering as atonement for sin. Excluding the Gospel of Mary and marginalizing the figure of Mary of Magdala worked to erase an important source for reconstructing early Christian women's theologizing and for advocating the legitimacy of women's leadership.

The 'revision' of Mary's history from apostle and prophet to repentant prostitute functioned on several fronts: it put Mary 'safely' into the confines of patriarchal definitions of women, it undermined appeals to her to support women's leadership, and it undermined the theology associated with her name. So while the canonization of Mary gave her a positive role as a disciple of Jesus and witness to the resurrection, it was a role in line with the needs and requirements of patriarchal theology and one which stopped far short of portraying her as an important leader in formative Christianity. The later conflation of her with the sinner woman in Luke and the adulteress in John fashioned a character even more pliable to patriarchal purposes, and further countered the powerful tradition of her as a visionary prophet and apostle. Yet at the same time, even the limited portrait of Mary in the New Testament has been a resource for women in their attempts to legitimate their practices of leadership.

Reconstructing a more accurate historical portrait of Mary of Magdala is not merely a matter of correcting the errors of Western canonical exegesis; it requires including all the extant source materials about her for consideration. All the sources, canonical and non-canonical, need to be read through the lenses of a feminist hermeneutics of suspicion which recognizes the politics of historicizing narratives or appeals to apostolic authority.

It should now be clear, too, that doing justice to the historical Mary of Magdala will require problematizing the canon as a starting point for both historical reconstruction and theological reflection. The portrait of Mary in the New Testament as a prominent disciple of Jesus and an important witness to the resurrection, although a positive portrait, is nonetheless a selective one. Mary of Magdala and women in general were not marginal actors in the formation of Christianity; their marginality was produced in part by the process of canonization as part and parcel of the theological development of 'orthodoxy' which condemned every early Christian theology that was supportive of women's leadership as heresy. Canon and 'orthodoxy' were devised in part to exclude women from positions of leadership and authority. They were not of course entirely successful. The invention of Mary as a prostitute has not kept women from appealing to her to legitimate their public preaching and teaching throughout the centuries. But insofar as it was successful, the cost has been high. A fuller and more accurate historical portrait of Mary of Magdala is one contribution toward rectifying that loss by providing an important resource for critical theological reflection and praxis.

Notes

1. See the study of traditions about Mary of Magdala by Susan Haskins, *Mary Magdalen: Myth and Metaphor*, New York 1993.

2. See John 8.1–11.

3. See Luke 7.36–50 conflated with John 12.1–8.

4. See Luke 8.1–3.

5. For a recent study of Mary of Magdala in the New Testament literature, see Carla Ricci, *Mary Magdalene and Many Others. Women who Followed Jesus*, Minneapolis 1994.

6. See Mark 15.40–41; Matt. 27.55–56; Luke 8.1–3; John 19.25; Gospel of Philip 59.6–9(?).

7. Mark 15.40–41; John 19.25; Mark 15.47 and Matt. 27.61 also place her at the entombment.

8. Mark 16.1–8; Matt. 28.1–7; Luke 24.1–10; John 20.1, 11–13; Gospel of Peter 12–13.

9. Matt. 28.9–10; John 20.14–18; Mark 16.9; *Epistula Apostolorum*.

10. John 20.17; cf. Mark 16.17 and Matt. 28.7.

11. For a fuller treatment of this process, see Haskins, *Mary Magdalen* (n. 1), 90–7.

12. *Against Praxeas*.

13. See for example, Origen, *Commentary on John* 6.37; 10.21.

14. Gregory, *Homily* 33. Quoted from Haskins, *Mary Magdalen* (n. 1), 96.

15. For an excellent extended treatment of these materials, see Anni Marjanen, *The Woman Jesus Loved. Mary Magdalene in the Nag Hammadi Library and Related Documents*. Nag Hammadi and Manichaean Studies XL, Leiden 1996.

16. One of the strengths of Marjanen's analysis is the clear distinctions he makes among the various portraits of Mary. She is not always shown to be superior to the male disciples; nor do texts which give her a prominent role necessarily treat women or female symbolization in a positive light (see especially his conclusions, *The Woman Jesus Loved* [n. 15], 216–25).

17. See the discussion by Elisabeth Schüssler Fiorenza, *In Memory of Her. A Feminist Theological Reconstruction of Christian Origins*, New York and London 1983, esp. 139, 304–7, 332–3.

18. *Dial. Sav.* 140.17–19. Text and translation in Stephen Emmel, *Nag Hammadi Codex III.5 The Dialogue of the Savior*, Nag Hammadi Studies XXVI, Leiden 1984, 80–1.

19. *Dial. Sav.* 139.11–13. Text and translation in Emmel, 78–9.

20. See *Dial. Sav.* 142.11–13, Emmel, 84–5.

21. See Matt. 28.16–20, Mark 16.14–20, where Jesus commissions 'the eleven'; the audience of Acts 1.8 is more ambiguous, saying only 'the apostles he had chosen' (1.2), but the Spirit clearly descends on a large group that includes both men and women (2.14). John is the least clear, saying only 'the disciples' (20.19–23).

22. See *Soph. Jes. Christ* III 98.10 (BG 90.1) and III 114.9 (BG 117.13). Text in *Nag Hammadi Codices III.3–4 and VI.1 with Papyrus Berolinensis 8502, 3 and Oxyrhynchus Papyrus 1081. Eugnostos and The Sophia of Jesus Christ*, Nag Hammadi Studies XXVII, Leiden 1991, 69, 169.

23. In *Soph. Jes. Christ* III 119.1–16 (BG 126.5–127.5), the Saviour gives them authority as 'Children of the Light' over all things, and the 'disciples' go out to preach. My translation, text, ibid., 177–8. Parrot's translation 'Sons of Light' is incorrect given the explicit presence of five women disciples (III 90, 17–18).

24. *Gos. Phil.* 59.6–11. Text and translation in Bentley Layton (ed.), *Nag Hammadi Codex 11.2–7*, Nag Hammadi Studies XX, Leiden 1989, 158–9.

25. See *Gos. Phil.* 63.34–36.

26. *Gos. Phil.* 58.34–59.6. Text and translation in ibid., 156–7.

27. For a more detailed discussion of this work, see Karen L. King, 'The Gospel of Mary Magdalene', in *Searching the Scriptures. Volume 2: A Feminist Commentary*, ed. Elisabeth Schüssler Fiorenza, New York and London 1994, 601–34.

28. Note, too, the correlative argument that knowing Jesus and receiving teaching from him are not in themselves sufficient. The *Gospel of Mary* takes to heart the many Gospel traditions which relate that the disciples around Jesus often did not understand him.

29. See *Gos. Thom.* I 14, *Gos. Phil.* 63.30–64.10; *Pistis Sophia* 11.71.2.

30. See Schüssler Fiorenza, *In Memory of Her* (n. 17), 3–95.

31. Mary of Magdala is not mentioned by name in the Acts of the Apostles, and seems to have disappeared from the scene, overshadowed especially by the male 'Twelve' and Paul. We might infer that the reference to 'the women' in Acts 1.14 includes Mary, but only Mary the mother of Jesus is named specifically.

32. See Acts 1.14.

33. Acts 1.21.

34. The use of the plural here is important, because an analysis of the texts in which Mary plays a major role shows a variety of theological positions (see Marjanen, *The Woman Jesus Loved* [n. 15]). The same is true, of course, for other apostolic figures as well. Peter, for example, is associated with theological positions supporting the physical resurrection of Jesus (for example, Gospel of John) and supporting a docetic christology (for example, the Apocalypse of Peter).

35. The Gospel of Mary clearly associates its theology with her not only by making her a central character, but also by ascribing the book to her.

36. I have suggested elsewhere that it is possible to identify certain elements that were common to early Christian women's theologizing (see 'Prophetic Power and Women's Authority: The Case of the Gospel of Mary (Magdalene)', in *Women Prophets and Preachers*, ed. Beverly Kienzie and Pamela Walker, Berkeley 1997, 21–41).

In Search of a Woman's Voice in Qur'anic[1] Hermeneutics

Amina Wadud

This article deals with two distinct yet reflective dimensions of female voice and the Qur'an: the female voice within the text and the female voice as commentator on the text. There are two purposes for this search for a woman's voice in Qur'anic hermeneutics, 1. to challenge the trend in the mainstream intellectual discourse in Islam[2] which marginalizes or denies the necessity and benefit of this voice, and 2. to expand the potential self-understanding among Muslims.[3]

Marginality of the female voice has become accepted by Muslim thinkers and laity alike as part of a divine decree.[4] Even if a woman is allowed the freedom to give voice in the form of commentary, she is prohibited from making an error. Such a prohibition is unprecedented. Not only have men made errors in their utterances, but also, the potential to err is a part of their graced condition as human beings. It has also been a part of their self-aggrandizement, implying that the human effort to come to understand the divine is legitimate only for themselves. Others, i.e. women, must remain mute.

As expected, women have also accepted this graced condition of men's humanity. We have accepted men as human, even while denying our own equal humanity. We have therefore accepted their denial of our right to give voice about the text, even to err. Not infrequently, however, error itself means variation from the established norm, or deviation. To avoid making such errors, women have turned to silence. Alas, this silence is a greater error, which limits the potential understanding of all humankind with regard to the text. The experiences of those who reflect upon the text for guidance helps to fulfil its divine claim. To know more about the text, all experiences with regard to it must be voiced and all voices must be listened to.

My search for a woman's voice includes the gendered person, woman, as well as the gendered essence, female. The female voice in the Qur'an is the voice of Allah,[5] and He is not a woman – nor even female. She is also not a man, nor even male. Both the male and the female voice are part of the divine venture to become known through text. As such, the divine voice synthesizes as well as transcends the dichotomy of male-female duality.[6]

Historically, the Islamic intellectual legacy has had a greater predilection towards Allah's male-like qualities, attributes and voice. However, these are not less important, nor more important, than the female-like qualities, attributes and voice. To correct the imbalance that has resulted from giving precedence to the male voice, Allah's missing female voice needs to be emphasized. Reverse hegemony is not however, the goal of this emphasis. The emphasis allows the full range of Allah's voice to reach the harmonious synthesis characteristic of the text and the Creator.

A precedented characteristic of religious history has been men's search for themselves and for guidance through which they validate their experiences. In the canon of the revelatory religions, female voices have been minimized. However, minimizing female voices is one way that human limitation is taken as divine. Divine intervention in the form of text cannot be equal to the limitation of human understanding. In the Islamic intellectual legacy, for example the entire fourteen centuries since the revelation itself, exclusively men have composed the works of exegesis. Naturally, this exclusivity effects our perceptions of the human self and the divine self. Despite this limitation, men have decreed that these exclusive male commentaries are definitive and authoritative.

Because the female voice of the text has been silenced, an Islamic ethos has developed which limits the potential of the text. This limitation does an injustice both to those who follow the guidance in the text and to the divine author of the text. For the text to expand towards its potential limitlessness, this impediment of interpretative authority must be removed. One help in removing such an impediment is by examining the female voice within the text and by increasing female commentary on textual meaning. Indeed the female voice must not only be given full utterance; it must even occasionally be given dominance.

The Qur'an is central to Islam, with an unprecedented consensus among Muslims as the primary source of all that is considered 'Islamic'. Despite this consensus, the text seems to be of less and less concrete consideration in the current intellectual, political, spiritual and moral resurgence of Islam globally.

My focus on the female voice and the Qur'an is part of a broader concern for regaining Qur'anic centrality in Islamic development. It gives voice to my personal and professional relationship with the Qur'an as part of this search for a woman's voice in Qur'anic hermeneutics and as a contribution towards the goal of regaining Qur'anic centrality.

My personal experience with the Qur'an

I became Muslim because the first time I went to a mosque I was wearing a long skirt and had my hair covered with a scarf. The disproportionate emphasis by Muslims on a woman's dress led those present to assume that I was ready for full surrender. Someone there said, 'If you believe there is no god but Allah, and Muhammad is His messenger, then you should make the pronouncement of faith-witness (*shahadah*: the first canon of Islam).' I did. With the *shahadah*, I began to fulfil the ritual requirements of a practising Muslim.[7] A few months later, I chanced upon someone who gave me a copy of the Qur'an. Only then did I really begin my surrender to the embrace of Islam.

As a child I used to love reading. It was my only true companion. I was not so much fascinated with story lines: saved damsels and courageous men. I was fascinated with words: words that gave meaning and dimension, words that spilled out over the pages and gave purpose and depth to my personal life of isolation. This primal characteristic of my life was especially touched by Qur'anic language acts.[8] How can a text with the intent and success of bringing about a global revolution in thought and action take the time it does to notice the pattern a leaf makes on its way to the earth?[9]

The Muslim historical and intellectual preoccupation with the text as a revolutionary message of social, political and moral importance has overlooked subtleties which the text itself has deemed important enough to include. It is not a hurried text, which relays an outward legal message and then moves on. Its poetic composition and aesthetic qualities inspire oral recitation competitions in various forms, world wide. Rendering Qur'anic passages in visual form helped to develop the art of calligraphy, one of five major features in Islamic art. Indeed, the aesthetic is a distinguishing characteristic of what it means to be human.

Ironically, recent Islamic resurgent movements have not sufficiently emphasized the significance of the aesthetic dimension of human faith and development. Such movements focus on laws and politics, instead of faith and hope. This may be one reason why the Islamic intellectual development has overlooked the female voice. Maybe it is not a plot for control of the one who nurtures. Can she be the one we fear? Or perhaps the female voice represents something so central and taken for granted in the landscape of Islamic ethos that paying specific attention to it seems uncalled-for.

Not only is the female voice included in the text; it makes a unique contribution to Qur'anic commentary. However, it is not only unique because it is completely absent in the Islamic intellectual legacy until this, the fifteenth century of Islamic history. The female, as one of many discussants, has no monopoly on the whole of textual meaning. No discussant can ever have. This article contributes towards the effort needed to correct the historical error of overlooking the female voice within the text and the unique perspective on textual meaning that women's experiences can contribute.

Qur'an and Muslims

Every day, millions of Muslims stand in ritual prayer reciting the opening chapter of the Qur'an. 'Guide us on the straight path' (1.6), it says. In the next chapter, the Qur'an responds, 'This is the book in which there is no doubt: a guidance for those who have *taqwa* (God-consciousness)' (2.2). In the prayer, Muslims ask for guidance, and the Qur'an pronounces itself to be that guidance, for all who have *taqwa* – not just Muslims, not just men – without a doubt.

The Qur'an is divine communication or revelation to humankind through the messenger Muhammad(s) for this purpose of human guidance. This is significant to the interpretative act. It establishes that the text must be read in order to follow its guidance. Every act of reading something communicated in language is an act of interpretation. Hence, it also establishes that interpretation of the text is necessary.

Every language act uses symbolic representations for meaning. A tree is a reality in nature, but the word T-R-E-E is only a symbol. Such a symbol is capable of modification in a manner completely unrelated to reality. By the simple inclusion of three letters, T-W-O, the number of the trees has doubled, without even planting a seed!

In order to make sense out of symbolic communication, one must specify the parameters of meaning for individual terms. Then each term must be related to its variant meanings within its syntactical constructs and textual context. Finally, language acts occur within a context of local meaning and application. How a reader or listener understands a language act reflects these three aspects: symbol, meaning and contexts. This aspect of interpretation is true for any communication between humans using language symbols.

The Qur'anic language act has an additional dimension: through a special communication method called *wahy* (revelation) it is divine communication to humankind. This further complicates the meaning-making process or act of interpretation. In order for the divine to communicate to humankind, the limitations of human symbolic communication must be compensated for, or overcome. Otherwise constraints are placed on divine meaning-making.

Languaging[10] and the Qur'an

The Qur'an states that it is 'a divine writ clear in itself and clearly showing the truth' (27.1). It does not use 'hocus-pocus' divine trickery to communicate divine wisdom for the purpose of human guidance. It uses language understandable to the Prophet, and to the people for whom it is intended as guidance (i.e. all humankind, according to the Qur'an). For the Qur'an to be clear, it can only use the symbols of ordinary human language. While human language uses various written and spoken constructs to communicate – sentences, phrases, paragraphs, similes, metaphors and parables, for example – it is still only words.

To include sacred meaning and ultimate relationships with only the one language medium poses the dilemma of divine text and constrains the interpretation of it. Our limitation as human interpreters cannot encompass all the infinitude of divine meaning. The language that we have for all aspects of creation, including the transcendent (*ghayb*: unseen), is the same language we use for the immediate (*shahadah*: the witnessed).[11] So religious language is multivalent: possessing various possible meanings, from literal to metaphorical. And the Qur'an explains that revelation includes allegorical statements (*mutashabihat*) and literal statements (*muhkamat*) (3.7).

One major consideration for Qur'anic exegesis is to determine which statements might be literal and which might be allegorical. The allegorical aspects of the text are necessarily the most difficult (or altogether impossible) to comprehend for the sacred-mundane relationship. Hopefully, other language acts in the Qur'an are more easily understood. However, 'one unique element for reading and understanding any text is . . . the language and cultural context' of the reader, which adds considerably to the perspective and conclusions of their interpretation . . . (R)eaders in different contexts (must) come to terms with their own relationship with the text.'[12]

The Qur'an includes statements specific to the context of its revelation in seventh-century Arabia and universal statements intended for all times. The relationship between the particular and universal statements have been variously understood in the history of exegesis. When the Qur'an uses women for examples, mainstream exegetes and jurists have restricted them as references for women only. In *Qur'an and Woman*, I have demonstrated the significance of women in the Qur'an as universal models[13] in contrast to this reductionism. One demonstration of this is Bilqis, the Queen of Sheba (27.20–44). Except for Prophets, Bilqis is the only figure in the Qur'an who is extolled for the quality of her leadership in terms of wisdom, spirituality and political acumen. Despite this Qur'anic precedent, many Muslims believe that a woman is prohibited from being a political leader.

Applying this universal application of Qur'anic discussion about Maryam (the mother of Jesus) proves more significant as a model of spiritual and moral guidance so that men will also focus on her experiences for lessons on their well-being. The language the Qur'an uses with regard to her supports this universal application. It describes her as among 'those' who have piety, who pray, or who have faith. However, it never uses the exclusive feminine plural form of the word 'those'. By using the masculine plural forms it includes males and females.

A woman's voice and the Qur'an

Except during the last two decades, there has been no substantial Qur'anic exegesis by a woman for fourteen centuries. In my own research I have been asked, 'Cannot men interpret the Qur'an *for* women?' There are ways in which men can interpret for women, just as there are ways in which women can interpret for men. But where this former proclamation realistically assesses the history of Islamic thought and Qur'anic exegesis, the latter is non-existent.

The Qur'an includes ultimate sacred postulates which can be confirmed by one reader for any other reader. For example, 'There is no god but the God (Allah)' remains true for all times and all places in the Qur'an. When men have interpreted the Qur'an, they have done so both for themselves as men and as human beings. Yet they do not distinguish themselves as men from themselves as human beings in the act of interpretation. When women interpret the Qur'an, they will also do so for themselves as human beings, as well as for themselves as women. Will women's interpretation make any difference to men?

In some ways, no one can interpret for any other. Each of us are limited in our context and against an infinite message. It is metaphysically impossible for any human to contain all of Allah's meaning in his or her interpretation. We are limited, while Allah is infinite. The two are not one and the same.

That Allah gave His word that He would provide guidance for all who have *taqwa* indicates an essential and dynamic relationship between divine infinity and human limitation. If we accept this characteristic of divine-human exchange, then each human effort to comprehend the text and implement its guidance is sincere and noble – albeit incomplete. Each effort reflects upon and operates within the constraints. All human discourse about Allah's epiphany through text is deficient, subject to time, place, gender, and other terms of the human condition.

In order for the guidance to remain relevant, it must be interpreted for every situation with the details of that situation in mind. The message is constant, divine, immutable, perfect, infinite. Understanding that message is specific, imperfect, constrained – but absolutely necessary for the message to fulfil its purpose.

The Qur'an confirms that males and females share in basic human-ness, but are distinct and equally important to humanity. Celebrating their distinction helps to fulfil some of the terms of the guidance itself. Yet, it simultaneously indicates that men cannot interpret *for* women, nor women *for* men. However, all human effort to interpret requires discourse between women and men as a necessary component for the best implementation of the text.

Although men have set themselves up as official interpreters of the text, they have discussed woman in the ways in which they have experienced her through need, want, love, hate, fear or indifference. They experience her from outside the centre of her own being. Despite this, men have given authority to their readings of the Qur'an. This authority implies that men are *real* people with full rights before Allah. Women can only be extensions of men. Men then serve women, whatever portion of the guidance they select as appropriate. It was also men who determined that a woman's voice is *awrah*.

Findings in Qur'anic understanding through a woman's voice

In Islam, any intermediary between worshipper and the Worshipped is prohibited. A similar prohibition should be placed on interevention between text and reader. All exegetes of the Qur'an agree that the Qur'an establishes absolute justice. Then justice is reduced to mean that men have absolute rights, and women have conditional equality. I approached Qur'anic exegesis on the basis of the Qur'an's claim of absolute justice.

In the Qur'an Allah states, 'We have created all things in pairs.' A characteristic of the created thing (*shay'*) is duality. Created things operate as a duality. Hence, males and females are of equal, distinctive and mutually complementary significance as part of the duality in creation. No *a-priori* significance can be given to one or the other.

Duality exists in more than just the oppositional form of dichotomy which works as an either/or polarization and which is presumed to apply likewise to the metaphysical realm. Such a dichotomy finds all of life existing in conflict. Pairs like male and female are presumed to be good and evil. If we removed the duality of nature from this linear polarity, we could address the genuine complexity of humanity. Good and evil are a part of all created things. The epistemological basis of this Qur'anic reading leads to a more dynamic integration of both/and.

Since Allah has both a male and a female voice, there is greater synthesis at the level of the divine. His male voice has been promoted as part of the privilege of being male: goal orientation, autonomy, hierarchy, dominance, action, authority and control. Allah's female voice has been underemphasized since it equates to those things shunned for being associated with the female: nurturance process, orientation, integration, synthesis, reciprocity, responsiveness, collectivity, cooperation. The outward reaching voice of Allah's *uluhiyyah* prioritizes, dichotomizes, dominates there by providing the necessary clear boundaries of contextualization. The inward reaching female-centred voice of Allah's *rububiyyah* synthesizes, integrates, suspends, thereby embracing the necessary ambiguity of life. In this, surely, the Qur'an offers the best of both worlds.

Notes

1. The Qur'an (pronounced Koran) is the holy book for Islam. It was revealed in the seventh century to an Arab Prophet named Muhammad Ibn Abd-Allah. It is considered by one billion Muslims to be the primary text of Islamic orthodoxy and orthopraxis. It has been preserved in the original form of its transmission by a detailed history of oral and written preservation. The tradition of preserving all or part of the book by rote memorization continues up until the present.

2. *Islam* is an Arabic word which means peaceful surrender to the will of God.

3. A Muslim is one who accepts the surrender to God.

4. A tradition has developed in Islamic cultures where the woman's voice is considered *awrah* (taboo). *Awrah* is a word used in the Qur'an exclusively for pudendum, the area of the body which must never been seen in public. Later mainstream Muslim thinkers applied it to a woman's voice.

5. 'Al-Lah' is a transliteration of the Arabic word for 'the God'.

6. This relationship of the Creator to duality in creation is discussed below, p. 43.

7. Among the ritual requirements of a practising Muslim is worship in a prescribed manner five times daily.

8. The gift of the Qur'an was made to me in 1973. More than twenty-five years later, it is the main focus of my scholarly career and academic research.

9. 'For with Him are the keys to the things that are beyond the reach of a created being's perception: none knows them but He. And He knows all that is on the land and in the sea; and not a leaf falls but He knows it . . .' (6.59). All Qur'anic quotations referred to will be referenced with the chapter number followed by the verse number.

10. Alton Becker, *Beyond Translation: Essays Towards a Modern Philology*, The University of Michigan Press 1995. Languaging is to be distinguished from language. Whereas language is 'the code image' and 'a system of rules or structures, which . . . relates meanings and sounds . . .', languaging 'combines shaping, storing, retrieving and communicating knowledge into one open-ended process' (9).

11. See Kenneth Burke, *The Rhetoric of Religion*, Boston 1961, 1–36.

12. Ibid., 5.

13. Amina Wadud-Muhsin, *Qur'an and Woman*, Fajar Bakhti 1992, 31–42.

Scripture, Feminism and Post-Colonial Contexts

Musa W. Dube Shomanah

Instead of the monologism implied in what is ironically called the Great Conversation – that is, the tradition of the Great Books: great white men talking to one another – we should move to establish what Johnella Butler calls 'difficult dialogues', models of cultural negotiation between opposing ends of the earth.

(Jerry Phillips, 'Educating the Savages', 40)[1]

Yet if you read and interpret modern European and American culture as having had something to do with imperialism, it becomes incumbent upon you also to reinterpret the canon in the light of texts whose place there has been insufficiently linked to, insufficiently weighted towards the expansion of Europe. But as a polyphonic accompaniment to the expansion of Europe, giving a revised direction and valance to writers . . .

(Edward Said, *Culture and Imperialism*, 60)

To speak of 'scripture', which means *'holy writ'*, or sacred writings, is to assume some of the following:

1. A social world-view that differentiates the sacred from the secular;
2. A literary form of texts as opposed to oral texts;
3. A literary canon that is regarded as normative;
4. The presence of religious institutions that are guardians of scriptural canons;
5. Particular forms of interpretation that befits a sacred canon.

This understanding of scripture is not applicable to all religious cultures of the world.[2]

Many cultures do not differentiate between the sacred and the secular, some do not have written scriptures, while some do not capitalize on the importance of written scriptures above the spoken or oral word, and many others do not have institutions that more or less guard the interpretation of their scriptural texts.

Feminism, on the other hand, describes a variety of women's movements whose concerns include analysing the social factors that legitimate gender oppressions of women, and devising several ways of liberating women. The relationship of scriptures and women is by and large problematic. First, the division between the sacred and the secular means that women, who are often identified with the negative side of most binary oppositions, are ranked with the secular. This social construction has been used to exclude women not only from religious institutions, but from public positions in general. Further, since scriptures often imply written texts, women have been largely excluded from their writing, selection, interpretation, and the religious institutions that guard their interpretation.

In biblical studies, one of the earliest feminist critics of the Bible as a canonical scripture was Elizabeth Cady Stanton. Elizabeth Cady Stanton categorically held that the Bible is a male book. Her conclusion was born out of seeing the Bible used to validate the social exclusion and marginalization of women. However, she was acutely aware that the Bible as a scriptural canon was more than just a collection of books. It also involves or depends upon institutionally directed interpretation that protects the integrity of the concerned text. To counteract the use of the Bible against women, both through its contents and interpretation, Stanton called upon women trained in biblical languages to interpret the Bible. The product of her feminist struggle with the use of the canonical books of the Bible to legitimize the oppression of women was what became known as *The Women's Bible*. This was a commentary which focussed on most biblical passages that dealt with women and reinterpreted them.

Given the continued use of biblical texts to marginalize women, and the continued male-dominated interpretation, Stanton's efforts were reactivated by women in biblical studies almost a century later. Women, who entered biblical studies in bigger numbers than before in the past thirty years, insisted on reading the Bible as women, for the liberation of women and all other oppressed groups. Feminist interpretations took various methods such as exposing the oppressive parts of the Bible, reinterpreting the negative passages about women, highlighting neglected passages that feature women, interrogating the language of God and the representation of women in the Bible, reconstructing women's history, reimagining the suppressed voices of women, etc. The early stages of women's biblical interpretation is captured in the following statement, that challenges and redefines the biblical canon: 'Whatever denies, diminishes, or distorts the full humanity of women is, therefore, to be appraised as not redemptive.'[3] This interpretative statement is an enormous challenge to the canonical authority of biblical texts, since authority is shifted from the written scripture and placed on the liberatory discourse of women.

One of the major projects that characterized contemporary feminist struggles with canonical scripture of the Bible was Schüssler Fiorenza's *In Memory of Her: A Feminist Reconstruction of Early Christian Origins.* Schüssler Fiorenza reconstructed the history of early Christian origins with the intention of placing women at the centre of Christian beginnings. This project included analysing not only the contents of biblical canonical books, but also the process of selection, compilation and subsequent interpretation of Christian texts. Schüssler Fiorenza found that the formation of the Christian canon was characterized by a male agenda that systematically excluded those books which featured women prominently, or gave them a significant position. She also found that the predominantly male interpreters and translators that followed through the ages marginalized the presence and contribution of women in Christian texts. These persuasive findings chipped away at the authoritative position of the Christian scriptures by showing that they are not or cannot be normative for all people.

The *Women's Bible Commentary* and *Searching the Scriptures Vol 2: A Feminist Commentary* encapsulate the feminist strategies of both using interpretation and restoring marginalized texts to deal with problematic canons. These strategies subvert the exclusive and oppressive biblical canonical scriptures. Simultaneously, they attempt to create an inclusive and liberating biblical canon. Both commentaries have engaged women of various backgrounds and methods to read the Bible as women and for the liberation of women. The latter commentary, in particular, makes a considerable effort to include and re-authorize 'women texts'[4] that were excluded and marginalized during the formation of the Christian canonical texts.

These feminist interpretative practices undermine the authoritative position of biblical scriptures by showing their inadequacy – their male authorship and perspective, their male-biassed compilation and their history of androcentric interpretation. Yet these feminist strategies are not meant to destroy or dispense with biblical texts. Rather, feminist biblical interpretation focusses on restoring the canonicity of the Bible by insisting that what is normative, what is the authoritative Word of God, is only that which embraces the liberation of women and, indeed, all the marginalized people of God. In short, authority is no longer within texts; rather, canonicity is measured by the liberation of women and all God's oppressed people of the world. Canonicity is God's justice or righteousness actualized and realized by God's creation at large.

Turning to post-colonial contexts, how are feminist canonical concerns and strategies of resistance related to the struggles of the Two-Thirds World colonized masses? I describe post-colonial contexts as 'all the cultures affected by the imperial process'.[5] That is, post-colonial cultures include those that were involved in and affected by Euro-American imperialism of the past four to five hundred years. Nevertheles, 'post-colonial' hereafter will refer to the colonized and their discourse of resistance as opposed to the colonizer. The term 'colonizing' will refer to 'the domination of physical space, the reformation of natives' minds, and the integration of local economic histories into the Western perspective'.[6] Post-colonial contexts are incredibly diverse; accordingly, the experiences of the colonized and their response to the colonizer assumed different strategies through time and space.

Studies in colonial and post-colonial texts find that empires are not only built or dismantled by the barrel of the cannon, but mainly by textual practices of writing and interpretation. Colonizing foreign races and their lands involves two intertwined literary practices. First, it involves a wide range of writing processes that represent the natives and their cultures as inferior, empty and in need of European civilization. These writing processes also involve normalizing imperial relations by creating literary settings that present dominating foreign people as normal and justified. Second, it involves a wide range of interpretative practices. Some of these include colonizing foreign spaces and people by perceiving the diverse cultures of the world cultures through a few Western canons, which are used to interpret all the 'strange' places and cultures. It also includes giving the natives the colonizer's literary canon to read at school and church, which in colonial times were mostly owned and run by the colonizers. Native texts are thus displaced or relegated to secondary positions, while the colonizers' texts are given an institutional privilege of representing the standard literature and religion. The imposition of the colonizer's literature on the colonized alienates them from their own languages, environments, cultures and people. The colonized are trained to yearn for the colonizer's places, religions, languages and cultures at large. *For a colonized subject to read, has been to identify with the colonizer* (emphasis mine). This is the colonization of the mind, for it alienates the colonized from their places and cultures, creating an immense identity crisis.

This use of Western canonical texts to colonize is discussed by Edward Said and Ngungi wa Thiongo. Said, who assesses the beginnings of comparative literature as a field of study, points out that it did not only begin in the high imperial times, but that 'when most European thinkers celebrated humanity or culture they were principally celebrating ideas and values they ascribed to their own national culture, or to Europe as distinct from the Orient, Africa, and even the Americas'.[7] In short, 'to speak of comparative literature therefore was to speak of the interaction of world literatures with one another, but the field was epistemologically organized as a sort of hierarchy, with Europe and its Latin Christian literatures at its centre and top'.[8]

Ngungi wa Thiongo also underlines that:

> it does not matter that the imported literature carried the great humanist tradition of the best Shakespeare, Goethe, Balzac, Tolstoy, Gorky, Brecht, Sholokhov, Dickens. The location of this great mirror of imagination was necessarily Europe and its history and culture and the rest of the universe was seen from that centre.[9]

Of course, this hierarchical promotion of European literary classics and its use to colonize included among them scriptural books of the Christian canon, the Bible. As Ngungi wa Thiongo points out, 'their greatness was presented as one more English gift to the world alongside the Bible and the needle. William Shakespeare and Jesus Christ had brought light to the darkest Africa . . .'[10] Similarly, Said holds that 'the displacing power in all texts finally derives from the displacing power of the Bible, whose centrality, potency, and dominating anteriority inform all Western literature'.[11]

In sum, Said and Ngungi's discussions indicate the following points. First, that colonization was historically linked to the sacred and secular canons of the West; second, that reading for the colonized was, and still is, largely to identify with the colonizer; third, that the Bible as a scriptural canon has been undoubtedly a colonial and colonizing book; and fourth, that the Bible belongs together with other Western secular classics.

The similarities of the post-colonial subjects' and feminists' concerns are evident. Post-colonial and feminist subjects are confronted with the struggle against reading canons they did not write or select; against literary images that derogate their humanity and legitimize their oppression; and against institutions such as the school, the church and the government that they do not control, which exclude their texts and impose texts that baptize their oppression. Both groups suffer from lack of language, alienation and oppression, etc. Their similarities are also evident in the methods of resistance adopted. They both learn and use the language and literature of their oppressors, but they reinterpret it, rewrite it, retell it, rearrange it to expose and subvert its oppressive representation. Post-colonial and feminist subjects both struggle to find their own languages and canons, by creating, retrieving or deliberately abrogating the languages of their masters instead of striving to write and speak them perfectly. Post-colonial and feminist subjects resist the denigration that is imposed on their cultures by insisting on the integrity of their literatures, oral traditions, religions and languages.

Yet there are also differences between post-colonial and feminist struggles against oppressive canonized texts. For instance, most post-colonial subjects initially adopted a strategy of restoring and preserving their derogated languages and literary canons. Feminists' early discourses, on the other hand, attacked most or all canons, declaring them to be oppressive patriarchal perspectives that need to be discarded, reinterpreted or replaced. The social location of earliest Western feminists' proponents, as the oppressed and oppressors, was also a problematic issue. In short, when Western feminists advocated the devaluation of all other canons, they were heard by many post-colonial subjects as echoing the practices of the colonizer, who also derogated the canonical texts of the colonized. Two-Thirds World feminists were often urged to privilege post-colonial concerns over patriarchal oppression.

Returning to the sacred canonical scriptures, how is the struggle of post-colonial subjects reflected in the work of Two-Thirds World feminist theologians? How does their struggle relate to the strategies of white Western feminists of the former colonizing centres? Lastly, if the various Western feminist theological practitioners begin to regard the Bible as both patriarchal and colonizing sacred canon, what are the useful strategies of resistance and restoring women's' sacred texts?

First, how do post-colonial feminist subjects deal with colonizing and patriarchal biblical scriptures? I believe the following quotations capture both the problem and the strategies of dealing with scriptures in post-colonial contexts. Mercy Amba Oduyoye and Elizabeth Amoah write that 'most Christians refer to Scripture as meaning the Hebrew Bible and its Christian supplement, the New Testament, but we would like to start with a reference to the "unwritten Scriptures" of the Fante of Ghana'.[12] They further hold that:

> All human communities have their stories of persons whose individual acts have had lasting effects on the destiny and ethos of the whole group. Such are the people remembered in the stories. Not all are Christ-figures; only those whose presence has led to more life and wholesome relations are commemorated as having been God sent.[13]

This approach retrieves and asserts the validity of the suppressed oral canons of the former colonized people of Ghana. The approach reflects the general post-colonial discourse of resistance and liberation. Yet Two-Thirds World feminists do not only engage in retrievals of their own suppressed native canons. They also reinterpret their own traditions, for they are also patriarchal. For example, although African women support the constructions of African christologies that affirm African traditions, yet 'at times they go beyond it or contradict it altogether'.[14] This critical stance is a response to both patriarchal traditions and their male interpreters, who sometimes force the maleness of Jesus in African traditions which included both men and women.

What is important here is to recognize that post-colonial feminists refuse to read the Bible as the only scripture, for it will be consistent with the colonizing approach that derogates or ignores all other world scriptures and canons. Like many other Two-Thirds World subjects, post-colonial feminist theologians insist on reading the Bible with and as one of the many world scriptures. Their approach underlines that the global post-colonial history makes it difficult for a reader to interpret the Bible as independent canonical scripture without subscribing to its colonizing history. Their strategy can be regarded as a practical application of what Edward Said proposes in the quotation at the beginning of this article and his book *Culture and Imperialism*. Said insists that since global colonization was effected through Western canons, it is imperative for today's readers to undertake a 'contrapuntal' reading of the cultural archive. That is, readers must 'begin to reread it not univocally but contrapuntally, with a simultaneous awareness both of the metropolitan history that is narrated and of those other histories against which (and together with which) the dominating discourse acts'.[15] In a statement that reflects these concerns and leads us to the second question, Kwok Pui Lan cautions that:

> Sisters from Asia, Africa, and Latin America would be unwilling to come if feminist theology is preoccupied with issues of the First or Second World. Other religious feminists, such as Jewish, Muslim, Buddhist, and Goddess-worshippers would be watching carefully what the Christian feminists have to say on the uniqueness of the Christian faith.[16]

Kwok Pui Lan is suggesting that since colonialism was effected through Christian texts and other Western canons, feminist theologians are obliged to realize first, that there are other sacred texts, and second, that the Bible now exists amongst these other scriptural texts of the world. Third, feminists are urged to read the Christian texts in such a way that they do not subscribe to their colonizing claims. Feminist readers must not focus on the patriarchal constructions only; rather, they must also identify and expose those texts that claim 'the uniqueness of Christian faith' as colonizing constructions, which authorize the suppression of other cultures.

In relation to the post-colonial struggles, the shortcomings of the Western feminist strategies to subvert the biblical canon are evident. For example, seeking to restore women to biblical scriptures, and showing that women were active participants in the spread of the early church, is a strategy that does not problematize the ideology of the Christian mission or try to re-imagine the mission. In other words, these strategies do not problematize the claims of 'the uniqueness of Christian faith', which when viewed from the post-colonial experience is tantamount to subscribing to the suppression of non-Western, non-Christian, non-white religious texts. The two feminist commentaries also maintain the uniqueness of the Christian faith. For example, *Searching the Scriptures*, whose approach is not only to engage various methods, readers and categories of analysis to interpret biblical texts, but also to restore the suppressed or marginalized texts that feature women, operates within the colonial canonical framework. First, its retrieval of texts generally presents the Bible as existing with extra-canonical texts of the ancient Graeco-Roman world. This strategy divorces biblical texts from its non-Graeco-Judaic, non-ancient contexts, where it was an effective tool in colonizing non-biblical cultures. Second, the restoring of suppressed 'women texts' that largely confines itself to the Jewish and Christian extra-canonical texts, ignores the voices of many in the Two-Thirds World, who are insisting on the integrity of their cultural texts and who are insisting that the Bible must be read together with, not apart from, or above, the cultures that it has been used to colonize.

Conclusion

Feminist and post-colonial discourses of resistance and liberation are an ongoing search for justice. Reinterpretation and restoring the suppressed 'women texts' is another way of confronting the use of biblical canonized scriptures that authorize the marginalization of women. But the post-colonial condition demands that feminist discourses must take cognizance of the history of imperialism and of how biblical texts and other secular canons of the West have been used to colonize Two-Thirds World masses. The latter factor demands that biblical canonical scriptures must be read with other world scriptures, be they oral or written. It demands that feminist reading practices identify, expose and arrest the colonizing construction of the biblical scriptures. Put differently, feminist theological discourses should be hybrid, since colonialism has indeed championed cultural contact.

While the patriarchal, imperialist and many other oppressive aspects of the various world scriptures are being addressed; while the suppressed scriptures of the colonized and women from multiple traditions are being restored and re-interpreted, the various feminist theological discourses must also enter and operate from the arena of the oral-Spirit aggressively. I say oral, because women's history and sacred words have remained largely unrecorded, although they have always been articulated. Instead of being seen as lamentable, this situation can be claimed as a space of speaking new life-affirming words. I also add Spirit, because it is a theological discourse that recognises divine partnership. The oral-Spirit framework can be a creative space, then, where women articulate their own sacred, life-affirming and liberating words of wisdom. In the feminist oral-Spirit space, responsible creativity that involves attentive listening to many oppressed voices and empathy; active prophecy that speaks against oppression and seeks liberation; and intent praying that seeks partnership with the divine, can begin to hear, speak, and write new words of life and justice.

Creativity in feminist circles has long been suggested.[17] Yet it is only too true that such a method has lacked the courage of application. To this day, we cannot boast of elaborate feminist re/writings of sacred texts from Africa, Asia, Australia, Europe and the Americas. The various feminist theological discourses have largely remained content with re-reading ancient patriarchal and colonizing scriptures. Thus, I would suggest that the oral-Spirit framework needs to be employed to invite women from diverse cultures completely to rewrite, create, hear, speak, sense and feel new sacred words of life, wisdom, liberation and justice. The oral-Spirit space needs to be employed to seek and to articulate life-affirming words, which speak justice with, for and to all the oppressed people. This, I would argue, is a necessary feminist theological step that will take both patriarchy, imperialism and other forms of oppression seriously in the scriptures of the world as well as allow women to speak their own sacred words. Simultaneously, it will also be a feminist theological step that seeks to open a space for cultivating dialogue and articulating liberation across the cultures.

Notes

1. In Jonathan White, *Recasting the World: Writing After Colonialism*, Baltimore 1993.

2. See Kwok Pui Lan, *Discovering the Bible in the Non-Biblical World*, Maryknoll 1995, 20–5.

3. Rosemary Radford Ruether, *Sexism and God Talk: Towards a Feminist Theology*, Boston and London 1983, 18–19.

4. I am putting these words in quotation marks because there is no conclusive evidence that extra-canonical books of the Bible featuring women prominently were in fact written by women.

5. Bill Ashcroft, Gareth Griffiths, Helen Tiffin, *The Empire Writes Back: Theory and Practice in Post-Colonial Literatures*, London 1989, 20.

6. V. Y. Mudimbe, *The Invention of Africa: Gnosis, Philosophy and the Order of Knowledge*, Bloomington 1988, 2.

7. Edward Said, *Culture and Imperialism*, New York 1992, 44.

8. Ibid., 45.

9. Ngungi wa Thiongo, *Decolonizing the Mind: The Politics of Language in African Literature*, London 1986, 18.

10. Ibid., 91.

11. Edward Said, *The World, the Text and the Critic*, Cambridge, Mass. 1983, 46.

12. Elizabeth Amoah and Mercy Amba Oduyoye, 'Christ for African Women', in *With Passion and Compassion: Third World Women Doing Theology*, ed. Virginia Fabella and M. A. Oduyoye, Maryknoll 1990, 35.

13. Ibid., 36.

14. Ibid., 43.

15. Said, *Culture and Imperialism* (n. 7), 51.

16. Kwok Pui Lan, 'The Future of Feminist Theology: An Asian Perspective', in *Feminist Theology from the Third World: A Reader*, ed. Ursula King, Maryknoll 1994, 63.

17. See Elisabeth Schüssler Fiorenza, 'The Will to Choose or to Reject: Continuing our Critical Work', in *Feminist Interpretation of the Bible*, ed. Letty Russell, Philadelphia 1985, 134–5.

II · Women's Sacred Words

Women's Lives as Sacred Text

Elsa Tamez

It is a notable fact that recent women's writing nearly always refers to their lives as a major resource for the work of feminist theology. Women from all over the world demonstrate this, obviously with differing accents.[1]

If women's experience is a major resource for the hermeneutic process of doing theology and reading the Bible, it is a logical next step to state that women's lives contain divine revelation. We can claim that the Spirit of God speaks to us and evangelizes us from the specific situations in which women suffer, struggle and overcome. We can even go further and say that the battered lives of many women show male-dominated patriarchal society to be sinful and in need of radical conversion (*metanoia*) if it is to be saved. And that is revelation.

Nevertheless, speaking of women's lives as sacred text marks a step forward from those above. In this brief article, I propose to set out some guidelines to help us understand such an affirmation. I shall begin with some clarifications on women and text, using some ideas drawn from semiotics on text.[2] I shall then distinguish two aspects: women's lives in sacred text and sacred text in women's lives. Finally, I attempt to analyse the meaning of women's lives as sacred text, and I conclude with the limitations and possibilities.

I. Women and text

Women are beings, living bodies woven from many strands. They are persons with their own stories – stories laden with anecdotes (sad and joyful, deep and trivial), plans, struggles and dreams. They are beings like all human beings. And yet we know that women are persons not recognized as such – free and with dignity – on account of their feminine gender as expressed in an androcentric, patriarchal and classist society. Their life stories, then, are either dismissed as inferior or passed over. This deplorable characteristic of their life story provides grounds for building a theological dialogue beyond generic declarations and absolute truths. This is why women often prefer to speak about women in order to avoid abstract generalizations.

Text is a tissue formed in the first place by its writer and then by its readers. A text also has its own story, beginning before its creation and extending after it in time. Its story will vary depending on its readers. A text can also have various stories, sad or joyful, hidden or manipulated, but those affected by it are always third parties. So the texture of a text varies; it can be smooth, rough, amenable, depending on the writer, the reader and the circumstances. A text, unlike a woman, has no life in itself. Life is bestowed upon it only when someone, a reader, introduces himself or herself into it through one of its many entrances. When this happens, it awakens and shows the reader its meaning through its signifiers and signifieds, its denotations and connotations, through, that is, all the meanings it produces and receives in this text-reader relationship. Intertextuality and intratextuality also contribute to the vitality conferred on it by another. The text is not a subject (actor) despite its interrelatedness. It will always be activated by third parties.

If it is true that erudite Arabic circles refer to a text as a body,[3] we might then say that text is body, just as woman is body. And in that a woman is a body made up of an infinite number of strands, a woman is also a text. But unlike a text, a woman is always a living text, even when she is asleep.

The strands of a woman's body mould her as feminine in sex. Woman is feminine text. The strands of the body of her text woven by her creator are not necessarily asexual: they could take the shape of a man or of a woman, depending on the socio-cultural conditionings of their artificer or reader. One sometimes hears 'This text is masculine', referring not only to the content or readable anecdote, but to the whole configuration of inter-related meanings produced by the linguistic sign. So text is body and body (of a being) is text, and there can be a deep relationship between them. This can be one of love or of hatred, of indifference or of domination, or simply of pleasure, as with poetic texts that make human bodies react as they delve into the deepest and most sublime sentiments expressed.

A written text qualified as sacred acquires a greater authority than any other text, including those that promulgate laws, since these can be changed. Sacred texts, once adopted as such, cannot be changed. As the establishment of the canon has defined their content, any possible changes will depend exclusively on interpretation, which is possible owing to polysemy and other literary recourses operating within the sacred text itself.

A text adopted as sacred also acquires authority over those subjects who adopt it as such. The degree of authority any text has exercised over these subjects will be seen in the practices, attitudes and visions engendered by the text. To which I would add that, since any text is highly subject to manipulation on account of its polysemy, the manipulation of a sacred text can lead to either life or death. So the relationship between women and sacred texts can be either positive or negative, depending on the life stories of both the texts in themselves and of the women.

II. Women's lives in sacred texts

The Christian sacred texts recount several women's lives.[4] Not many, since the texts were produced in a patriarchal and androcentric culture in which women were considered inferior to men. Nevertheless, thanks to these texts, some women's lives have been eternalized and remembered across many centuries.

The texts contain the life stories of some women who really surprise us by the way they escape from the framework of patriarchal society, such as Deborah and Judith; they also recount other stories of less spectacular women, who have nevertheless been fixed in memory through being mentioned. And many other women are mentioned very much in passing, usually dependent on and subject to a patriarch, husband or son. Nevertheless, the text goes its own way, and its polysemic character lays it open to various interpretations; these, by concentrating on the words and syntax of life stories, can produce a richer sense of women's worth, revealing more meanings than the author had in mind and these in confrontation with the patriarchal system. There are stories, however, that eternalize the sadness and marginalization of women, as well as the violence done to them. Phyllis Trible has called these 'texts of terror'.[5] These are texts whose strands take on a dominative masculine texture, and the texts – accomplices in this – offer no alternative interpretation that calls their violence to account. The only – limited – way out is recourse to other passages in the sacred text that point in a different direction.

So, then, in reproducing women's lives, the play of words as linguistic signs, the text, can sometimes become the women's accomplice by bringing out their value, or it can remain the accomplice of the patriarchal society from which the writer comes. The production of meanings is beyond the control of the writer.

The biblical scholar Carlos Mesters insists on the close relationship that exists between the 'book of life' and the book of the Bible.[6] In other words, we can say that there are two sorts of women's lives that engage in dialogue, one their actual lives and the other their lives in the text. In this sense it is correct to state that women, as readers with life stories, reactivate[7] the text in reading the life stories of women in the Bible and – to a certain degree – enrich the lives of these women in the sacred text. And when they come to the texts of terror they simply activate these as such so that patriarchal society may be ashamed.

There is a limiting factor in sacred texts, as in any text, in that the women's lives reproduced in the sacred texts have a border. However much their meaning can be enriched, the persons concerned have frontiers they cannot cross. Through the texts being closed off, the women's lives in sacred text are silenced once they reach the border in all senses. Neither their actions nor their words can be changed, however much one would wish to do so.

III. Sacred text in the lives of women in history

Once a text is adopted as sacred, as we have seen, there is an unequal relationship between those who adopt it and the text itself, since this has the task of showing itself as canon. And in traditional understanding, canon implies subjection and obedience.

Over the centuries, women's lives have been impacted by sacred text, sometimes in a positive way and sometimes in a negative one. In many cases the impact has been deadly. As the society in which the text was produced and present-day society are both patriarchal, the androcentric statements in the text are raised to the rank of absolute truths. Through this, both societies reinforce one another, with the aggravating factor of legitimation on the part of the sacred. The text is then raised against women of all times in order to subject them and confine them to the rank of inferior beings. The text thereby does violence to women; the sacred text is imposed upon the text of life, the canonized body upon the body existing in time.

When this happens, the text becomes an accomplice of readers with a patriarchal and androcentric mentality. The plurality of meanings in the text is covered over, and anti-woman declarations are extracted as dogmas read denotively. Conservative interpreters, authorized by officialdom, close off lines of inquiry in order to seal away meanings in the text that could produce a different word. Women then fail to become reading subjects who can activate the text and awaken other discordant meanings; they remain dependent on listening to what is said about the text, regardless of what the text might say through its reserve of meanings.

But the opposite also happens, has done throughout history, and is doing so even more in recent times. The sacred text has also become the accomplice in uprisings. It has impacted on the lives of women rendered invisible by their miserable situation and turned them into beings capable of being protagonists of their own story. By recreating the story of women in the Bible the sacred text has come back to life in the actions, attitudes and dreams of many women today. They manage both to appropriate the text and to struggle against it when it sets itself against them as the accomplice of patriarchal society.

When a sacred text collaborates in giving women their dignity, there is a mutual fulfilment: the woman is fulfilled under the impact of the sacred text, and the sacred text is fulfilled through being revealed as truly divine. God, spoken of by the sacred text, is made manifest in the dignification of all God's creatures. Written revelation is then seen to lead to this dignification.

There is, however, still a limiting factor. The sacred text often stops short of the life experience of present-day women. As it was established many centuries ago, it cannot take account of all modern situations. The Spirit of God enclosed in the canonical text transcends this text and constantly seeks to express itself through other texts and other bodies, in writings and living beings.

IV. Women's lives as sacred text

In the process of investigating the scriptures, speaking of women's lives as sacred text is important because of the limitations just mentioned. As the texts are composed using formulas written and inscribed hundreds of years ago, they necessarily present us with frontiers that are now impossible to cross. Cultural categories, for example, are eternalized in accounts of women's lives of different periods. Connotations and meanings have their limits through being in some way always tied to the body of the text.

The lives of present-day women can be influential in increasing the meanings to be found in the text: they can even, with some hermeneutical daring, change history to some extent, or perhaps continue it. Nevertheless, the logic of the text will indicate what is to be expected, and the anecdote with its personages will anchor its readers.

The other limitation mentioned is more obvious: there is an enormous distance between the sacred text and the present century. The text, through stemming from a human experience of a particular time and place, cannot take account of all cultural and socio-economic situations, let alone of later scientific developments. It stops short of the reality experienced by women today.

The greater problem, though, is that the text, produced in a patriarchal society, risks annihilating women when it is adopted as sacred, when patriarchal and androcentric statements are raised to the rank of dogmas.

We women have done no more than enter on a hermeneutical struggle by collecting texts that favour women and objecting to those that oppress them. This is why we have to go beyond the sacred text and look for the Spirit of God made manifest in other texts, living or written.

At the beginning of this article I tried to establish a symbolic relationship between text and women. I said that the text is a woven tissue and that women are also made up of living tissues: women are body and the text is body. This comparison enables us to make a bridge of dialogue between the two more or less even sides of women and text. But as we are dealing with a sacred text, we have to introduce qualifications. The written sacred text stands above the woman text. The sacred text is truly a privileged space. Women, too, are concerned to re-read it constantly in order to draw new practices and attitudes from it, to look for new ways forward, to find dignity – to feel God. Of course they cannot find all this in texts that damage them. But despite these texts they often insist on re-reading and reconstructing the texts of the sacred text. This is because they believe they contain divine revelation.

It is at such moments that a relationship we might call 'intratextual' is established between women's lives and the life of the text. Carlos Mesters' 'parable of the door' describes this perfectly in speaking of the poor who go in through the door of the house of the Bible as though it were their own house and come out of it without realizing they have come out.[8]

Beyond this, as women's bodies are not just any bodies but those that form both the object of and the conscious witness to systematic and fortuitous violence and discrimination, we also have to introduce qualifications with regard to them. God's option for the excluded puts them in a special position. We might say that women's bodies also 'spark off' sacred, epiphanic spaces. Their personal and social sufferings, their struggle against the structural sin of the patriarchal society that appears in all circumstances of life, and their faith in the possibility of men and women living together worthily, fruitfully and in mutual respect, relate a whole history of salvation that deserves to be listened to. These women's life stories also bring the insensitivities of the salvation history written in sacred texts and codified by tradition into the open.

The analogy of woman as sacred text is capable of overcoming all the above-mentioned limitations. If the structure of the text limits meanings by closing itself off each time it is re-read, women's body-tissue-text has the possibility of remaining ever open, even to themes not dealt with in the sacred text. Furthermore, we know that the dove of the Spirit flies where it wills and alights on bodies other than that of the written text. We need to point out what the sacredness of women can derive not only from written text but directly from God. God can be revealed directly from women's bodies, their sufferings, struggles, joys and utopias.

Women's bodies, then, can manifest themselves as sacred text setting out their stories to be read and re-read and to generate liberating actions and attitudes. Women's lives enshrine a deep grammar, whose morphology and syntax need to be learned for the sake of better human inter-relationships. For Christian women, when women's lives 'tell' or reveal something similar to the liberating story of Jesus Christ, the human face of God, there is sacred text. It is a new story, since it transcends that related in the Synoptics, because it is reworked with new categories suited to the actual situation. When we read of crucifixion in the framework of women's bodies, there is sacred text, because we are reading of struggle, grace and sin. When we read of dignity and achievement in women's lives, there is epiphany of God, even when we read stories of pleasure not told in the Bible.

We can go a step further. I have said that text-woman is living, unlike text-text. Now this vitality allows it to transcend any text, since it not only recreates the written text but produces new personalities, images and scenes never before heard or seen, with the capacity to show themselves as sacred texts. The beneficial interrelation between the canonical sacred text and the lives of women as sacred text gives free rein to new productions. One clarification, though, has to be made: *not all of women's lives is sacred text; nor are the lives of all women.* Just as there is no revelation of God in texts that discriminate, there is likewise no revelation of God in those women's lives that show hatred, envy, violence, disrespect and subjection of one to another.

At this point it might well be asked what difference there is between woman as text and other living texts of a different nature which also suffer marginalization and violence and struggle against them. The question is to the point: a similar parallel could in fact be made with the life stories of black and indigenous people. The only difference is that women's lives run through all societies and cultures; oppression of women is found in all the various cultures, as is their struggle against it.

In conclusion: relating the sacred text to women's lives as sacred text is a beneficial formula both for women and for the sacred text. On the one hand, it helps to give written sacred text back its character as such, since it reactivates dignifying texts and disqualifies *with authority* those that discriminate. On the other, God's revelation in sacred texts inspires women *with authority* to recognize their lives as being sacred, as something to be cared for and defended. And finally, women themselves – their life stories – manifest God who challenges the whole of society, men and women, to live as creatures made in the divine image and likeness.

Translated by Paul Burns

Notes

1. Cf Letty M. Russell (ed.), *Feminist Interpretation of the Bible*, Philadelphia 1985; Ursula King (ed.), *Feminist Theology from the Third World: A Reader*, London and New York 1994; Pilar Aquino, *Nuestro clamor por la vida*, San José 1992.

2. As a starting point, and only as a starting point, I shall make use of some concepts from Roland Barthes' *The Pleasure of the Text*, 1990, and Umberto Eco's *Opera aperta*, without sticking closely to their propositions and even distancing myself radically from them. What matters here is the search for a way into speaking of women's lives as sacred text.

3. Barthes, *The Pleasure* (n.2).

4. The plays of the text transcend stories, or anecdotes; here, however, I concentrate on them in order to bring out the relationship between women's lives in the text and women's lives at the present time.

5. Phyllis Trible, *Texts of Terror*, Philadelphia 1984.

6. Carlos Mesters, *Defenceless Flower*, Maryknoll 1989; *Por trás as Palavras*, Petrópolis 1977.

7. The text is like a television set, which has to be switched on to produce images. The reading a person makes of the text is like a light switch.

8. Mesters, *Por trás as Palavras* (n. 6), 13.

The Slave Narratives and Womanist Ethics

Joan M. Martin

'I'se saved. De Lord done tell me I'se saved. Now I know de Lord will show me de way, I ain't gwine to grieve no more. No matter how much you all done beat me and chillen, de Lord will show me de way. And some day we never be slaves.'[1]

These words, uttered by an ex-enslaved[2] blackwoman[3] from the pages of a slave narrative, speak of the experience of the African American community in slavery. They speak about the nature of womanhood, the understanding of relationship to God-Jesus-Holy Spirit, and the nature of moral agency by enslaved and ex-enslaved women in the struggle to realize human wholeness and freedom in a two-hundred-and-forty-year period. Although less than twelve per cent of the slave narrative corpus was produced by women,[4] this body of literature has become a primary source discovered, recovered and critically used by womanist theologians and ethicists in making claims regarding the authentication of blackwomen's historical and contemporary religious experience as well as community survival. Womanist theological and ethical praxis endeavours to speak of a multi-dimensional tradition within African American Christianity both in the Black Church tradition and in the academy. Further, womanist scholars challenge these traditions in the light of the real lived experience of blackwomen as theological thinkers and moral agents in the face of internalized racism, sexism, patriarchal heterosexism and classism.

I want to focus on the slave narrative as sacred text in the African American community, and how it provides a legacy of and 'witness' to both the collective faith story of African Americans and the individual faith journeys of women. A crucial part of this focus is to see the slave narrative as a historical text and witness, and, when about and by women, a gendered text.

The slave narrative as historical source

The slave narrative is a source of enslaved 'witnessing' which can be characterized both as an individual document and as a wide-ranging, broad corpus of autobiographical and narrative writing. The genre includes journals, newspaper articles, magazine interviews, church records, personal letters and amanuensis autobiographies (those dictated to another) of ex-enslaved women and men. Slave narratives are one of the foremost instruments for revealing the institution of slavery as this was experienced by enslaved men and women in their struggle for freedom in the antebellum[5] United States.

Enslavement in the North American British colonies began in 1619. The long process of enslaved testimony began in 1703 and culminated in 1944. During this period, slave narratives took on specific purposes which varied in different historical eras. For many of those written or dictated from 1703 to 1830, the narrators sought to expose the social prejudice which they endured, a prejudice that was not limited to their economic status as slaves but was fundamentally based on skin colour and the wider conditions of servitude. A second historical period, coinciding with the last period of the antebellum from 1830 to 1865, saw a different purpose in the slaves' use of narrative. It took on the purpose of propaganda and of political entreaty in the abolitionist movements, both black and white. The enslaved, in flight to the North, now utilized his or her narrative to attack the institution of chattel slavery as the root problem, not, as before, society's understanding of the nature of skin colour and supposed racial endowments.

The third and last period of slave narrative extends from the post-Civil War and Reconstruction[6] period to 1944. In it, we find narratives representing several different purposes. In the Reconstruction period through the early twentieth century, many narratives are presented as reminiscences of slavery in order to remind the reader of the struggle of African American women and men, the continuing need for justice, and the urge for racial self-improvement and progress. Women narrators, in particular, often hold up the memory of the slave mothers (who, in many instances, were their own mothers) and condemn the hypocritical standards of purity, delicateness and refinement by which the African American woman was judged. Still other narratives provide the opportunity to espouse strategies by which blacks could live within the confines of Jim Crowism following Reconstruction, and accommodate the reality of race relations of the late nineteenth through the mid-twentieth centuries.

Thus, the slave narratives provide a 'continuous record of that institution'[7] which reveals a legacy of struggle for self-expression by humans considered to be non-humans. These pages exemplify the thought, language and action of those yearning for legal, political, social, religious and economic rights required for human dignity – those at the time the country termed 'chattel'. In the face of pro-slavery apologetics and white normative social history, the resilience of the slave narrative as historical documentation unveils the perversity of American life caught in the continuing perniciousness of its white racism.

New perspectives on the lives of enslaved women

Blackwomen historians have deepened our historical understanding of enslaved women's lives in particular. They are doing their work with a dual focus: (*a*) the reclamation of blackwomen's history of slavery from blackwomen slave and ex-slave sources, and (*b*) a black-orientated gender analysis of black and white male sexism, patriarchy and white female racism. Their findings claim that African American enslaved women embodied the paradoxes of oppression as found in a multi-focal location of antebellum slave ideologies concerning sex, race, gender and class. Further, the nature of this blackwomen's embodied, enslaved existence is a unique centre and point of departure for defining the slave existence more fully. For both sexes, black female and black male, the general lifelong condition of slavery had many similarities. However, it had its sharp and marked differences as well. The enslaved blackwomen's experience is very particular and distinguishable from that of her male counterpart, and includes:

1. the distinct nature of enslaved women's work life and her life in the slave quarter – family and social;

2. the nature of enslaved women's forms of resistance, sabotage and insurrection for self and community against slavery which include religious belief;

3. the African culturally-oriented sensibilities used in enslaved women's transformation and creation of slave culture in the midst of a more dominant and oppressive slaveholding white culture;

4. the high degree of gender consciousness and racial solidarity which enslaved blackwomen developed; and

5. the fullness of creativity in the midst of forced labour, and the dreams which enslaved women had for themselves and their children, reflected in African American enslaved culture both in its strength and in its weakness.

Two narrative examples demonstraate several of these points. Katy, a fifty-year-old woman, escaped from her master in Virginia. Many years earlier, Katy's husband had been beaten to death by their master for his resistance to the master's sexual advances toward Katy. In a newspaper article, Frederick Douglass writes that,

> The murder left Katy a widow with two girls of ten and twelve years old. It also raised up in her a determined resolution to break away and be free, and hereupon the latent energy of her nature came into powerful action. She knew that money was indispensable so she worked and toiled between tasks [so much so] that their virtuous resistance caused her master to increase in [his] severity, and [she], by trafficking with the negroes around, accumulated a small sum. But it took twenty years to do so![8]

From the narrative of Aunt Sally, 'The moment that [I] was free to act for [myself], with what spirit and energy did [I] take hold of life.'[9] Reports like these were prominent in interviews, articles and newspapers.

The slave narrative as sacred text

The fundamental issue I want to address is that of the slave narrative as sacred text. For black liberation theologians and womanist ethicists, the slave narrative is a departure for the African American Christian tradition in the context of the 'invisible institution'.[10] By highlighting the nature of enslaved Americans' relations to the cultural setting of Africa, the theo-ethical orientation of enslaved women in the antebellum becomes more clearly focussed. I draw on the notion of an African heritage of common orientations[11] as found in contemporary anthropological and historical fields. Such notions assist in understanding the hospitable attitude that many enslaved Africans had toward the spiritual and communal orientation of Christianity. Emphasis was put on communal life as the source of a person's individuation, and on the active relationship between the dead (ancestors) and living persons as a core of moral harmony. There were also orientations that accommodated the cultural forms and content of others rather than resisting or destroying such elements; they permitted the appropriation of sacred and secular power. Such orientations can be seen as the patterns which help in identifying the cosmological reference points of enslaved African Americans as revealed in the slave narrative.

However, Christianity became a religious battleground between the slavocracy's attempt to define and control slaves and the enslaved African/African Americans' self-definition of their humanity and religious viewpoint. Seen in the light of this struggle, the slave narrative has a crucial dimension. *Slave and ex-slave testimony bear witness to the power of God's Spirit.* God's Spirit is revealed authoritatively in the scriptures, but continues in post-biblical times to be God's agent. Slave and ex-slave testimony expresses the enslaved ones' intimate relationship with Jesus, and her/his belief in the sustaining power of prayer. Slave and ex-slave testimony proclaims that the purpose of God was not slavery, but freedom. Such testimony shows how enslaved African Americans acted daily and decisively, in large and in small ways, as moral agents in response to their religious conversion and commitment to God's call to faith and freedom.

In the Works Progress Administration (WPA) Slave Narrative Collection, the ex-slaves' testimony clearly demonstrates that slaves did not believe that slavery was the will of God.[12] Sarah Ford told a WPA interviewer, 'Law[d] me, de heaps of things go on in slave times what won't go on no more, 'cause de bright light come and it ain't dark no more for us black folks.' Ford goes on to recall how Old Uncle Lew was preaching one day about how the Lord made everyone 'in unity on one level'; the next day, the slave master heard about it, and put Old Uncle Lew out in the field with the rest of the slaves.[13] The imagery of 'bright light' contrasted to the 'dark' may sound like internalized racist language to this generation of blackpeople. However, two hermeneutical references are clear. First, Ford draws upon the biblical imagery of 'bright light' and '[the] dark', and interprets freedom and slavery respectively in this fashion. Second, the imagery unmistakably refers to the Good News that enslaved women (and men) had in God, especially in the midst of the evil of slavery which could punish a person for preaching a theology other than that of the slave master.

The female narratives of the antebellum period likewise understand that the peculiar institution was a peculiar *human* institution, not one divinely sanctioned. Here, the nature of causality and the ability of God to be revealed through faith becomes exemplary. In the midst of the degradation that enslaved peoples experienced, many knew and attested the fact that only God and other members of the enslaved community turned a sympathetic ear to their troubles. Old Elizabeth, born in 1766, wrote that at the time of separation and sale from her mother as a young girl, 'I had none in the world to look to but God, [so] I betook myself to prayer, and in every lonely place I found an altar.'[14] In the life of an enslaved woman, separated from one's kin and slave community, the remainder of the world was a hostile place. It was a world of slave and slave master. In such a context of isolation, it was clear to enslaved women that God was different from, and not associated with, the cruelty and perversion of chattel slavery. God was, instead, a sheltering reality.

How the slave narrative has acted as sacred text within this African American religious tradition is fundamentally a hermeneutical question. I have suggested that the origin of the hermeneutical event and the productive reading[15] of the text relates to: (*a*) the African roots of the

African American Christian experience, (b) the historical event of slavery, (c) the slave narrative as a written text, and (d) the hermeneutical task facing womanist theologians and ethicists in the light of the contemporary African American Christian community. The nature of the text – its naming and departure point – is the historical encounter of African Americans with the institution of chattel slavery. This is a historical experience giving occasion for the written discourse – the slave narrative. This experience is concretized in the narrative and reflects not only the individual narrator but the *collective narration of the signified event over a prolonged period of time.* In essence, the slave narratives were the creation of a people telling a story which incorporated fundamental understandings shared by enslaved people throughout the antebellum period. It is in this collective experiential nature of the narrative – oral and written, in expressing faith journeys, clandestine worship, fervent prayer, and ultimate hopes lifted to God – that the slave narrative approaches 'sacred text'.

The model presented by biblical scholar Walter Harrelson is helpful in this regard.[16] Harrelson's concern is to establish features of Israelite biblical literature which combine to create a tradition – a central core of fundamental understandings or content that is more than a mere theme or set of motifs, and is detectable in a process of handing down. Further, 'it should be possible to identify its basic themes, the motifs that articulate the themes, the plot that emerges, and the tradition as something to be received and handed down intact'.[17] According to Harrelson, the salient characteristics of a tradition are:

1. It is received from others and transmitted further, especially from one generation to the next;

2. It has both form and content . . . remaining formal for purposes of retracing it;

3. A tradition is the immediate property of a group or a community, that is, has a direct function for the people who transmit it;

4. A tradition is 'living', developing, malleable and only relatively stable; it can become changed and reinterpreted to meet the needs of its transmitters;

5. A tradition is usually oral but can also be in written form as long as it fulfills the other criteria mentioned here, especially that of being able to develop and adapt; and

6. It tends to be cumulative and agglomerative.[18]

These features provide a means of appropriating the notion of sacred text for the slave narrative without claiming that it has the same stature as the Hebrew-Christian scriptures. One of the African features retained by

African Americans was that part of their religious world view was a sense of the unity of the cosmos in which all was viewed as sacred, and in which different religious practices could be accommodated harmoniously. This understanding pervaded the life of the individual, both internally and externally, and was applied as well to the social and natural world. Hence, it makes sense that the enslaved understood him-and-herself in a universe alive with the power of God. Accordingly, ex-slave Carey Davenport reported that:

'When darkies prayed in slavery they darns't let the white folks know 'bout it or they beat them to death. When we prayed we turned a wash pot upside down to the ground to catch the voice. We prayed lots in slavery to be free and the Lord heard our prayer. We didn't have no song books, the Lord gave us songs. When we sing them at night 'round the fire place it would be just whispering like . . . so the white folks not hear us. We would hum them as we wo'ked in [the quarter] in the field, walking to town.'[19]

Compressed within this testimony is a myriad of theological meanings that witness to slavery days, to the nature and necessity of dangerous worship in a so-called Christian country, and to the unity of religious life in spite of the reality of slavery. An outstanding dimension of this testimony is the extent to which slaves would go in order to worship God. They faced beatings, many of which resulted in death. Another ex-enslaved woman, Ellen Butler, said it this way, 'Massa never 'lowed us slaves to go to church . . . they done that way cause white folks didn't want slaves to pray.' Obviously, this enslaved woman intimated that whites feared the power of religion to incite the enslaved to rebellion or to sustain possible notions of freedom through religious practice. This kind of response is found throughout the antebellum period.

Slavery is the event from which sacred witness to God arises, and the event from which the sacred text, the slave narrative, is created. In 1975, James Cone wrote:

The story was both the medium through which truth was communicated and also a constituent of truth itself. In the telling of a truthful story, the reality of liberation to which the story pointed was also revealed in the actual *telling* of the story itself.[20]

'Story' is then an important religious component in the slave narratives which makes them a critical source for the historical grounding of blackpeople's experience of God. Through the slave narrative *their story of faith*, enslavement and hope for freedom finds voice. Through this story, womanist theologians and ethicists can discover non-formal doctrines of the nature of faith and examines the role religion has and can play in oppression and struggles for liberation. The 'story' foregrounds African American theologians' and ethicists' constructive task and liberatory praxis. This is so true that the vast majority of contemporary black and womanist theologians and ethicists affirm that 'the black church begins in slavery . . . and thus slave religion provides the first source for [any] contemporary statement on black theology'.[21] The slave narrative, as blackpeoples' story of slavery and blackpeoples' voice in faith and struggle, tells us how the enslaved defined their humanity and their religion.

In conclusion, a terse story in Sojourner Truth's narrative illustrates the slave narrative's deep expression of the enslaved African American story of faith in God's power to overcome the adversities of life and of slavery. It is a story which moved abolitionists – white and black – when told in the settings of the antebellum anti-slavery movements. Today, it could serve as a powerful story for the sustaining of African American women and others who may be struggling to reclaim their children from the inhumanity of county jails and state prisons, from public-assisted foster care and the courts, and from the street gangs and alley drug wars of US cities.

'I tell you. I stretched up, and felt as tall as the world. "Missus," says I, "I'll have my son back again!" She laughed. "You will, you nigger? How you goin' to do it? You ha'nt got no money." "No Missus but God has enough, or what's better! And I'll have my child again."'[22]

Notes

1. Norman R. Yetman (ed.), *Voices from Slavery: The Life of American Slaves – in the Words of 100 Men and Women who Lived It and Many Years Later Talked About It*, New York 1970, 228.

2. Enslaved is a term referring to the status of a person who, through the coercion of law and practice but not personal choice, is the chattel property of another person. I use it rather than 'slave', which denotes the person as being rather than the condition of servitude. Enslavement is used to indicate the coercive institution, and is used synonymously with 'slavery' and 'slavocracy' as the institution and ruling ideology of the pre-Civil War southern United States.

3. Blackwoman is a term I use to indicate identity more accurately instead of using 'black' as an adjective of 'woman'. 'Blackwomen' connotes the social construction of race and gender as well as the interrelationship and inseparability of the experience of being a black adult female in a racist, sexist and classist society.

4. John Blassingame, *Slave Testimony: Two Centuries of Letters, Speeches, Interviews, and Autobiographies*, Baton Rouge 1977, xli.

5. Antebellum – the name for the period of US history prior to the Civil War. Likewise, postbellum is the period immediately following the Civil War. Both are also used as adjectives.

6. Reconstruction – the postbellum period of reorganization and reestablishment of the southern states that had seceded from the Union at the beginning of the Civil War. The period included some economic redevelopment, new federal and state constitutional amendments and laws enfranchising the rights of blackmen, and a measure of federal troop protection for freed men and women (the ex-enslaved). When Reconstruction ended, most southern states reinstituted discriminatory laws and practices against African Americans in a system called 'Jim Crowism'.

7. Marion Wilson Starling, *The Slave Narrative*, Washington, DC [2]1988, 1.

8. *Douglass' Monthly*, Vol. 1, no. 8, January 1859.

9. Aunt Sally, *Aunt Sally, or The Cross The Way of Freedom: A Narrative of the Slave Life and Purchase of the Mother of Rev. Isaac Williams of Detroit, Michigan*, Cincinnati 1858, reprinted 1969, 92–8.

10. Albert J. Raboteau, *Slave Religion: The 'Invisible Institution' in the Antebellum South*, New York 1980, ix.

11. In using the term 'African heritage of common orientations' I follow the suggestion of Lawrence Levine and refrain from using the term African 'survivals' or 'retentions'. Levine notes that the latter two terms prejudice the issue, prior to its discussion, and posits orientations as mere vestiges or quaint reminders of an exotic culture enough alive to make it picturesquely different but not substantial. See L. Levine, *Black Culture and Black Consciousness: Afro-American Folk Thought from Slavery to Freedom*, Oxford 1977, 34. Also see George Brandon, 'Sacrificial Practices in Santeria, an African-Cuban Religion in the United States', in *Africanisms in American Culture*, ed. Joseph E. Holloway, Bloomington 1990, 143; and Sidney Mintz and Richard Price, *Birth of African-American Culture: An Anthropological Perspective*, Boston 1976.

12. Cheryl J. Sanders, 'Liberation Ethics in the Ex-Slave Interviews', in *Cut Loose Your Stammering Tongue: The Slave Narrative in Black Theology*, Maryknoll, NY 1991, 103–36.

13. George P. Rawick (ed.), *The American Slave: A Composite Autobiography* (41 vols), Westport 1972: *The Texas Narratives*, Vol. 4, Part 1, 44.

14. Elizabeth, *The Memoir of Old Elizabeth, a Colored Woman*, Philadelphia 1863; reprinted in *Six Women's Slave Narratives*, The Schomburg Library of Nineteenth-Century Black Women Writers, ed. Henry Louis Gates, Jr, New York 1988, 4.

15. For a discussion of a theory of reading as production, see J. Severino Croatto, *Biblical Hermeneutics: Toward a Theory of Reading as the Production of Meaning*, Maryknoll 1987.

16. Walter Harrelson, 'Life, Faith, and the Emergence of Tradition', in *Tradition and Theology in the Old Testament*, ed. Douglas A. Knight, London 1977, 11–30. Harrelson draws on the work of Douglas A. Knight and Josef Pieper.

17. Ibid., 18.

18. Ibid., 14–15.

19. George P. Rawick (ed.), *The American Slave* (n. 13), Supplement 2, Vol. 4, 1052.

20. James Cone, *God of the Oppressed*, San Francisco 1975, 57.

21. Dwight N. Hopkins, 'Slave Theology in the Invisible Institution', in *Cut Loose Your Stammering Tongue* (n. 12), 1.

22. Sojourner Truth, *The Narrative of Sojourner Truth* [1850 edition as dictated to Olive Gilbert], ed. with introduction by Margaret Washington, New York 1993, 31.

Women as Originators of Oral Scripture in an Asian Society

Saroj Nalini Arambam Parratt

Introduction

When Western scholars write of religious traditions other than Christianity, they tend to interpret them in terms of concepts and thought forms accepted in the Western world. These concepts are but the products of Western traditions and cultures which are usually very different from those of other traditions and cultures. Even the Western concept of 'scripture' is the result of a long period of understanding and interpretation, in which an originally oral tradition came to be written down and accepted as the record of the acts of God within a specific historical context. The idea of 'scripture' therefore should not be understood exclusively within the categories which presuppose Western cultures and traditions. Rather, we have to use categories which are indigenous to each particular culture. In many cultures these categories are those of oral literature, and consist of spoken liturgy, spontaneous oracle, songs or hymns, and myths.

In the Meitei religion, the spoken or sung liturgy and the spontaneous oracle are the most important forms of 'scripture'. Both are the prerogatives of the *maibi* (priestess), the female religious functionary, who has a pre-eminent role in Meitei religion.

The Meitei

The state of Manipur is situated on the north-eastern border of India with Myanmar and comprises 8500 square miles. Its population is around 1.8 million, of which the Meiteis comprise above two-thirds. It is surrounded on all four sides with nine ranges of mountains, and the heartland of this state is the fertile valley which is the home land of the Meiteis. The Meiteis have a highly developed culture with an extensive written literature in the ancient Meitei script dating back a thousand years or more.[1] Written and oral traditions trace the settlement of the various sub-groups which now constitute the Meiteis into Manipur back to the beginning of the Christian era. They brought with them a complex religious system, much of which remains intact today.[2] By the middle of the eighteenth century, however, enforced Hinduization took place during the reign of Garib Niwaz.[3] There was never, however, a complete take-over of Meitei beliefs and rituals. Significantly, Hindu restrictions on women were never adopted.[4] Conflict between the indigenous religion and Hinduism continued until a synthesized form of religion emerged.[5] Meitei religious beliefs and practices have never been abandoned, and today a revitalized Meitei religion has become a popular focus for ethnic identity. At every important stage of life, as well as in crises, Meiteis turn to their indigenous faith. The *maibis* play a prominent role in this, for they have preserved the cultic practices and act as guides through their oracles.

Meitei religion focusses on the worship of the *lai* (deities, divinities). Though there is a high God (Atingkok), he is almost a *deus otiosus*, and his spouse Leimaren (Supreme goddess) is far more important. Leimaren is associated with the earth and with the waters. She is the source of the oracles which are uttered by the *maibis*. As such, Leimaren is regarded as the progenitress of the primeval *maibi* (*Khabi*), whose spiritual descendants all *maibis* are.

The performance and the ritual word

Of all the Meitei religious ceremonies, the *Lai Haraoba*, literally 'Pleasing of the gods', is the most important. In this, the beliefs, expectations and hopes of the people are reflected.[6] This festival takes place at the commencement of the rains and is performed by the area or locality; it may last as long as thirteen to fifteen days. On a smaller scale it can also be performed by the family group. In this case it is called *Lai Chaklon Katpa* (literally, the offering of the meal to the *lai*), may be performed at any time, and lasts just one day. But in both cases the essence of the ritual is the same.

Lai Haraoba is a vast and complex festival, which has grown up over a long period of time and incorporates several disparate rituals. Perhaps the most important of these is the giving of oracles. The main maibic oracle takes place on the first day as the *lais* in whose honour the festival is being celebrated are symbolically 'called up' out of the waters.[7] The officiating *maibi* crouches beside the water, immersing the *leiyoms* (ritual packets symbolising the *lais*) with her right hand, and ringing a hand-bell with her left. Her face must be covered. She first sings the praises of the *lais*, and then invokes Leimaren to give her the oracle:

You, Mother (Leimaren) . . .
On this round crown, on this head rest[8] be seated awhile;
Give us your oracle clearly, clearly discerning one strand of hair from
another.[9]
From deep down within the navel,[10]
Give me good tidings:
Do not give me tidings which are old,
But give me tidings which are new . . .
I, the priestess of the primordial earth, am your servant.

As the possession begins to take hold, the *maibi*'s body begins to shake
violently; she 'sees' the *lai*, and utters the oracle. After the oracle is
completed, the *lais* are symbolically taken out of the waters as the *leiyoms*
are placed in earthen pots and taken in procession to the shrine.

The maibic oracle

The oracle comes from the goddess Leimaren to the female *maibi*, never
from a male *lai* to a male *maiba* (male priest). The dominance of the female
religious functionary in the pronouncement of the oracle is characteristic of
Meitei religion. The symbolic language used of the oracle describes the
lai as 'sitting upon' the *maibi* as the rider controls the horse, and the *maibi*
as being linked by the navel to the Mother goddess through the umbilical
cord. On subsequent days of the festival the giving of the oracle is repeated
each morning, but now at the shrine, after the offering of flowers and fruit
have been made.[11]

The oracle may be for the benefit of the individual or the people who are
performing the *haraoba* or the whole nation, and may take the form of a
blessing or a warning. There is, however, always a message to an individual
who makes an offering.

The content of the oracle

The content of oracles varies.[12] In the case of oracles of communal warning, the recipients may consult among themselves or seek further clarification from the *maibi* on how to implement what was required. As the
Meiteis are traditionally an agricultural people, often the oracles contain
messages about the abundance of crops or cattle, or of human fertility. Con-
versely they may be about epidemics, pestilence or flood. Formerly, during
the period of Manipur as an independent kingdom, oracles would also
concern matters of national peace and security, and the long life of the king.

Oracles follow a set formula in which the *lai* speaks in the first person, e.g. 'I will bless/protect you', or 'I will avert the calamity/destroy the enemy'. This is then followed by a command to make a specific offering. On the individual level the oracle may promise fame or success, warning against an adversary, or simple foretelling of the future. Occasionally the oracle may pronounce that help is not possible as the individual has reached his or her allotted life span.

The term used for the oracular command where an act of offering by the person concerned is involved is *katchouhei* (from the verb *katpa*, to offer), or *toujouhei* (from the verb *touba*, to do). The suffixes -*chou* and -*hei* are a verbal form used by the more powerful to a subordinate (e.g. such as the king would use to his subjects). But the recipient of the message is left free to choose – it is not the ought as a categorical imperative; it is a favour given by the *lai* to the one who obeys. The *lais* have given humans a freedom to choose. The relationship is not a demand but one of mutual give and take. There is thus an element of love and friendship underlying the demand by the superior to the subordinate. The *lai* is not so much a punisher but a guardian and protector.

The implication is that though there may be adverse forces, the *lai* has the power to overcome them for the people. But the choice is left open to the people. On the other hand there are also cases where a person has transgressed the *lai*'s command. In this case the oracle will declare the *lai*'s righteous anger and reprimand unless the right appeasement and acknowledgement of the wrong is made.

Oracles therefore link up right behaviour with personal, social and political blessings and suffering. As in ancient Israel, which was vulnerable to calamities of an agricultural and political nature, so also the maibic oracle in Manipur gives guidance as to the right behaviour on the part of the people in matters affecting social and individual safety and prosperity.

Thus, though the form of the oracle is fixed by generations of tradition, its content is varied.[13] In this the *maibi*'s function is not just related to prosperity or calamity, but to the people's existence and survival as a people. It has a very important role on the existential level.

Specific cases of oracles

There are many cases of maibic oracles which related to events in the history of Manipur. Before the last world war, for example, oracles given at *Lai Haraobas* throughout the country warned of times of death, famine and conflict, and even of the enemy who would come from the east. Along with this was the word of consolation that Manipur would not be completely destroyed.[14]

Other oracles spoke of individuals. In 1891, shortly after the *de facto* assumption of control of Manipur by the British, an oracle spoke in enigmatic terms of the defilement on a golden plate by a fox, an unclean animal. This was interpreted as referring to the taking of a Meitei princess, Sanatombi, by the then British Political Officer, Col. Maxwell.[15] Oracles thus had a distinctive role in national life, and could even be used as a form of political protest.

Attempts at canonization and male control of the oral tradition

Traditionally there are three main forms of the *Lai Haraoba*, and there are also three schools of *maibis*. Additionally, the *haraoba* in honour of the different *lais* of specific areas or clan groups uses varying praise names in the texts. Recently, however, there has been a twofold attempt to marginalize the female *maibis*. The first is the assumption of the role of the *maibi* by male *maibas* without the cross-dressing which was mandatory in the past. The other is the attempt to canonize the oral text of the *Lai Haraoba* into a written form, and thus to standardize the varied forms used in the different forms of the festival. This move is being made by the institution of the *Pandit Loisang*, the 'institute of pundits'. All the pundits (a term derived from the Sanskrit Hindu tradition and not from indigenous Meitei culture) are male, and they are neither *maibas* nor male *maibis*.[16] They have begun to take part in performances of the *Lai Haraoba* as 'instructors'. This represents an attempt by males to take over the religious authority of the *maibis* and to assume control of the oral tradition. It is an attempt to form a fixed sacred canon, controlled by male scribes. This will result in a univocal in place of an interactive multivocal oral text. Sacred discourses in fact are under threat. If it succeeds, the freedom which the *maibis* have as the mouthpiece of the *lai* will be lost, and free inspiration will be stultified. Religious authority will be transferred from charismatic female leaders (the *maibis*) to a body of male scribes, thus marginalizing the female mediums. This tendency is probably to be attributed to a form of patriarchalism which is ultimately derived from Hinduism, and which is quite at variance to the clear pre-eminence of the female in Meitei religious tradition.

Conclusion

Meitei religious tradition regards the supreme female goddess, Leimaren, as the source of creation and of the sacred word. This word is mediated through the priestesses, who function in this respect as charismatic proclaimers of the word of the *lais* for public and private good. Despite the resurgence of Meitei religion within recent decades, contrary trends are afoot in some circles which would seek to reduce charismatic inspiration in favour of a formal written text, and subjugate the female *maibis* to male non-charismatic control. Such trends not only threaten the integrity of the Meitei religious tradition, but also are contrary to the modern movement for the freedom and dignity of women. If this movement continues, it may result in the decline of the maibic oracle, and the destruction of the social balance between the sexes in the Meitei society.

A ritual text represents the voices of the past. When, as with the Meiteis, such ritual texts leave space for modifications and additions, they also reflect the present. However, once a text becomes fixed there is no room for modification. When this happens, though the text remains a reminder of the past, its continuity with and relevance for the present will be threatened. Such texts do not speak *directly* to the present situation. Oracles, however, are the voices of the sacred text of the present day, and both ritual text and oracle depend upon their reception and participation by the community.

Notes

1. *Cheitharol Kumbaba* (State Chronicles) (edited by L. Ibungohal Singh and N. Khelachandra Singh, Imphal 1987) and *Ningthourol Lambuba* (edited by O. Bhogeshwar Singh, Imphal 1967) are especially significant, as they throw light on the history of the people.

2. For a discussion of Meitei religion see S. N. Parratt, *The Religion of Manipur*, Calcutta 1980.

3. See S. N. Parratt, *Garib Niwaz, Wars and Religious Policy*, Internationales Asienforum 20, 1989, 295–302.

4. Thus there has never been child marriage, dowry, restriction on widow remarriage or sati in Meitei tradition, and women have considerable economic and social prestige and power.

5. See J. Shakespear, 'The Religion of Manipur', *Folk Lore* 24, 1913, 109–55, also Parratt, *The Religion of Manipur* (n. 2), 167–79.

6. For a full analysis of the *Lai Haraoba* festival and commentary on the oral text see S. N. Parratt and J. Parratt, *The Pleasing of the Gods: Meitei Lai Haraoba*, New Delhi 1997.

7. In the ritual of *lai ikouba*, calling up the *lais* from the waters, the *maibi* holds two small ritual packets (*leiyom*, one each for the male and female *lais*), which consist of the buds of the *langthrei* plant wrapped in layers of banana leaves. These are attached to cotton strings (*hiri*). The *lais* are symbolically drawn up through the strings and at the end of the ritual the *hiris* are wrapped around the *leiyoms* and placed in earthen pots for transportation to the shrine.

8. The headdress is a plaited cloth such as is used for carrying pots.

9. I.e. discerning the smallest detail.

10. Possession is regarded as located in the navel, and the 'pulse' in the navel increases during the possession.

11. Traditionally a male might rarely be called to be a 'male *maibi*': in such cases he must wear the female dress of the *maibi*, should speak and act as a female, and is addressed as '*ima* (mother) *maibi*'. The essential femaleness of mediumship is not compromised.

12. E.g. the oracle might declare: 'Such and such a person has done this or that, and in doing so had not respected my (the *lai*'s) will and command; and so I intend to punish him/her. But if he/she offers the (stated) appeasement, then I will forgive and save him/her.' In the same way the oracle might declare: 'Such and such an enemy is intending to destroy such and such a person/family/the whole country: but I the *lai* will save you and will protect you.'

13. Though the *maibi*'s invocation of the goddess to give her the message is more or less a set formula which has been handed down for generations through oral tradition, even in this set form there is room for slight modifications by adding phrases. For example, there was an interesting addition in a recent *haraoba*: the goddess was addressed as 'Mother Leimaren, who gave birth to the Meiteis' (*Ima Leimaren, Meitei pokpi*). This addition seeks to emphasize the resurgence of ethnic identity over against greater India.

14. During the last world war, Imphal, the capital of Manipur, was turned to a battlefield where hand-to-hand combat took place between the Japanese and the British and Allied forces, and where the Japanese advance was finally halted.

15. For an account of the events leading to British control of Manipur and Maxwell's role see J. Parratt and S. N. Parratt, *Queen Empress vs. Tikendrajit: the Anglo-Manipuri Conflict of 1891*, New Delhi 1992.

16. See n. 11.

Performing Sacred Texts

Yuko Yuasa

I. Introduction

My theme is the performance of sacred texts. As my special field is creating biblical Noh dramas, I challenge the notion of 'scriptures as a bounded book of fixed and closed canons' to be used as a didactic tool. My understanding of scriptures is that of Miriam Levering: 'a special class of true and powerful words, formed by ways in which these words are received by persons and communities'. Thus liberated from a conventional notion, I explore the domain of Japanese sacred texts expressed in the performance and texts of Noh drama, searching for liberation and transformation. My aim is to share the findings with readers.

I am often asked at my presentation, 'Why do you take all the trouble to write, produce and show biblical Noh dramas to people in and outside Japan?' In the course of this article I hope to answer this question. I broadly follow the feminist spiral method of Letty Russell, touching the four areas of experience (texts), analysis, tradition (the Bible) and transformation (biblical Noh drama), and advocate the full humanity of women together with men. References are only selectively acknowledged.

II. Ameno Uzume: sacred texts in the Japanese tradition

Japan has two written records of the formative days of the nation, *Kojiki* (Record of the Ancient Matters, 712 CE) and *Nihonshoki* (The Chronicles of Japan, 720 CE), which are collections of myths, legends and embryonic history. Both writings include two stories of a dynamic leader Ameno Uzume. She is the first recorded singer/dancer/goddess, to whom most performing arts of Japan today trace back their roots. The gist of the first story is retold thus:

The supreme sun goddess, Amaterasu, had withdrawn into a cave after being frightened by certain barbaric actions of her brother, Susanowo. As a result, darkness, death and destruction reigned, and the myriad gods and goddesses of the heavenly field gathered to establish a plan for enticing her out of the cave. The action chosen was an elaborate gathering of sacred symbols and offerings, the chanting of liturgical prayers, and performance of a ritual dance by Ameno Uzume. The ancient myth describes the scene.

> Ameno Uzume, binding up her sleeves with a cord of the heavenly Hikage vine, tying around her head a headband of masaki vine, and binding together bundles of bamboo leaves to hold in her hands, overturned a wooden bucket in front of the heavenly rock-cave door, and stamped resoundingly upon it. Then she became divinely possessed, pushed down her garment to expose her body.

The effect of this performance was the wild laughter of delighted gods and goddesses. Amaterasu, hearing this laughter, opened the rock-cave door to look out and asked, 'Why are you dancing so merrily?' 'Because, O Supreme Amaterasu,' Ameno Uzume answered, 'we have found another supremely divine being beside you'. The sun goddess was shocked, and at that very moment, strong gods took the hand of the sun goddess to draw her out of the cave. Thus light, life and order were restored.

The second story of Ameno Uzume concerns the expedition of Ninigi, the grandson of Amaterasu. The gods and goddesses of the Heavenly Field decided to establish a colony in a distant land. They dispatched many messengers to the proposed land demanding surrender, but each time the messengers were either killed or returned injured. At last they decided to send the supreme goddess's own grandson. This time a host of powerful attendants followed the special messenger. And Ameno Uzume, renowned for her wit and charm, was included in the group.

> At the junction of heaven and earth, they ran up against a giant. His mouth shone red, and his eyes were as bright as the Yata-mirror. No one dared look at him, let alone to talk with him. Then Ameno Uzume was called up to negotiate with him. 'You are good at dealing with such people. Go ask him what he is doing there.'
>
> Once again, Ameno Uzume, having opened her garment, came forward and faced him smiling.
>
> 'Why are you doing this to me?' asked the Giant.
>
> Ameno Uzume asked back to him,
> 'Who are you, standing in front of the party of Amaterasu's grandson, I dare to ask you?'
>
> 'As I heard that the sun goddess's grandson was on the way, I have come to welcome him. My name is Sarutahiko.'

So she asked the giant to be their guide. Having arranged for the safe journey of the band, the character Ameno Uzume then disappeared from both books (hand in hand with Sarutahiko, according to S. Tsurumi).

III. Analyses of the texts

Who is Ameno Uzume? There are two important roles that Ameno Uzume, the legendary primeval singer/dancer/goddess, plays in *Kojiki* and *Nihonshoki*, the earliest literary works of Japan. In the first story the displeased supreme leader, Amaterasu, locked herself in a heavenly cave, plunging the world into darkness and disorder. Ameno Uzume succeeded to luring her out of the cave and restoring light and order to the world.

The second story concerns the confrontation between heavenly travellers and a menacing giant. When her troupe hesitated, Ameno Uzume alone, unintimidated, greeted the earthly giant and opened a way of negotiation. In both cases her approach was to open up her garment to expose herself, inviting laughter and disarming the aggressive nature of both parties.

The characteristics of Ameno Uzume demonstrate some important principles of feminist leadership and methods of implementation, in the face of crisis. She has laughter within herself and power to invite others' laughter. She calls upon hidden resources when confronted with the formidable authority of the opponents. The vulnerable and non-violent character of her action is her strength. She overrides the storming waves with good humour. When darkness and anxiety hangs over the community, her vibrant nature and vivacious manner empower others. Her optimism transforms despair into hope.

Ameno Uzume's method of implementation is performance. She uses her body movement and the power of eros. Because of her dynamism she is trusted by the group and, in turn, the people's reliance is the source of her energy. She represents the common people at a tribal level, inspiring others by her humanity and acts of courage rather than attempting to impose authority from a position of political power.

Noh drama traces its roots back to Ameno Uzume and her performance in front of the rock-cave door. This mythic origin empowers Noh actors/actresses. They are sustained by the primal energy that dispels evil through ritual art. In a Noh drama, *Miwa*, Ameno Uzume dances to free people from despair, allowing light, life and harmony to reign.

IV. Miriam, a biblical counterpart

True to the feminist spiral method, this section relates the theme of Ameno Uzume to the Bible. Miriam, the prophet and the sister of Aaron, is chosen as her biblical counterpart, because of the similar position of leadership. Miriam appears in five passages in the Old Testament (Exodus 2.1 and 15.20; Numbers 12.1; 12.9 and 20.1).

In Jewish legend Miriam is symbolically associated with water. In the story of baby Moses, an unnamed sister arranges for him to float in the Nile past Pharaoh's daughter. She watches from a distance as his basket is retrieved safely. She comes forward to the princess and offers to find her a nurse from her Hebrew women, to the effect that she brought Moses' mother to nurse him. By the resourcefulness and prudence of this act, the prophet Miriam is presumed by tradition to be the unnamed sister.

Following the triumphant Red Sea crossing, Miriam is introduced by name, and called a prophet. Miriam is the first woman to be called prophet. Her prophecy and vision are mentioned only briefly, due perhaps to editorial bias, or because of the manner of the expression of her vision: performance of the sacred texts by song and dance. The transient impact is difficult to record. Miriam's words may remain intact in Exodus 15.1–21, as some scholars believe, in the entirety of a poem called the 'Song of the Sea' attributed to Moses. Textually, only a modest refrain recorded in Exodus 15.21 is attributed to Miriam.

Though brief, Miriam's words contribute to feminist leadership. She said after criticizing Moses' marriage with a Cushite woman, 'Has the Lord spoken only through Moses? Has he not spoken through us also?' It was a critical time for a leadership challenged by uprisings and usurpation, as the Hebrew name for the Book of Numbers suggests, '*bamidbar* (in the wilderness)' describing an unsettled landscape of chaos, darkness and disorder. Miriam never denies Moses' authority. Her recognition of Moses' voice is indicated by 'also'. She points to multiple leadership.

Miriam, like Ameno Uzume, led the people by song and dance. The effectiveness of her leadership is as great as her Japanese counterpart. Miriam took a tambourine in her hand, 'and all the women went out after her with tambourines and with dancing. And Miriam sang to them: "Sing to the Lord, for he has triumphed gloriously; horse and rider he has thrown into the sea"' (Exodus 15.20–21). Miriam led the women at the Exodus in dance to celebrate the end of their slavery in Egypt. Doug Adams discerns, in a late Beshallach Midrash, that 'dance is linked to a forgetting of and freeing from the troubling past' (Diane Apostolos-Cappadona, *Dance as Religious Studies*).

Dance focusses our attention on our physical nature. As we notice the limitation and strength of our body, we reflect on the way God created human beings. When we think of the material need of life, we understand the grace of God who is willing to give us God's own life. The meaning of the incarnation becomes clearer to us. This leads to a deeper appreciation of sacraments, particularly the eucharist, eating and drinking God's flesh and blood, in a worshipping community.

The energy given by physical movements such as breathing, voicing, shaking off pressure and dancing, is functional in transforming perspectives. Experiencing the liberation from the past by dancing, with such powerful leaders as Miriam and Ameno Uzume, people are led to recognize that life is not determined by the old self. This realization of one's being born anew gives us a hope, preparing us for faith in the resurrection. The joyful experience of dancing invigorates us to welcome the Holy Spirit, moving in tune with the cosmic energy.

V. Hannya Miriam, a transformation into a biblical Noh drama

The fourth part of the feminist spiral method is 'transformation', after the analyses of the mythic text of Ameno Uzume and a theological reflection on Miriam. A creation of a biblical Noh drama with Miriam as a heroine fulfils the requirement of transformation. The Noh stage is the setting for our drama. The Noh stage symbolizes the cosmos. The stage is this world. The mirror room behind the curtain is the other world. A narrow corridor bridges the two worlds. The pine tree painted on the back wall is a sacred ladder where divine beings descend.

Hannya Miriam

Type: Dream Noh with two masks: Hannya (a demon mask) and Zo (a goddess mask).

Sources: (1) Bible: Exodus 2.1–10; 15.1–21; Numbers 12.1–16, Psalm 30.12.

(2) Noh: *Ama, Aridoshi, Miwa.*

Theme: Miriam is the protagonist of this drama. She is Moses' sister, and one of the few woman prophets officially recognized in the Bible. Whereas Moses is recognized as one of the high-ranking members of the community, Miriam is without official status or rank. Moses is sometimes remote and aloof, while Miriam is always among the people. She was instrumental in freeing the people from the suffering of slavery, and led them through the wilderness to the promised land.

At one point she was stricken by leprosy as a punishment for criticizing Moses. For seven days she was shunned from the camp. Despite her expulsion, people supported her. The whole congregation paused in their journey and refused to continue until she was able to rejoin them.

The mask of Hannya expresses Miriam's torment. The mouth displays her anger, whereas the eyes are filled with tears of sorrow. Underlying this suffering is a protest against heaven's injustice and an appeal for compassion.

The climax comes when Miriam is redeemed through God's grace. Her sorrow is turned to joy. At the end, God's glory and triumph are proclaimed. Miriam celebrates with her song and dance. Her Hannya mask is changed into a Zo mask. Her hymn is accompanied by the voice of the people, represented by the chorus and the audience.

Points of interest: This play has two sources of inspiration: the biblical passage about the prophet Miriam, and the fourteenth-century Noh dramas *Ama* (the Diver) and *Miwa* (Mt Miwa). The heroine of *Ama*, like Miriam, overcomes adversity. Both women exhibit great courage and endurance, challenging powering forces with self-sacrifice. At the end, both heroines, having triumphed and being redeemed, sing and dance in praise of God.

Symbolism of this play: Miriam always appears together with the motif of water. Its essential symbolism is life. Miriam's role was to support the people's life in the desert. She was a mediator between God and the people. She fulfilled this role through dance and song.

According to Kino Tsurayuki, to move heaven and earth one does not need force. Love, expressed as poetry, will bring tears to the eyes of demons and will unite the hearts of men and women.

Both cultures value individual effort, the need for freedom, and responsible expression of the religious spirit. The heart is the source of this personal truth which finds expression in poetry and dance.

VI. Performance of biblical Noh dramas

The past experience: There have been five performances of my biblical Noh drama on different themes, dating from 1995 till the present. The most recent occasion was on 12 September 1997 in a Methodist church in Birmingham, England. It was organized by Rev. Dr Lee Hong-Jung of the Centre for North East Asian Mission Studies of the School of Mission and World Christianity, Selly Oak Colleges. About sixty people, members of the church congregation and theological students from Asia, Europe and USA gathered in the end-of-the-summer-holiday campus. The production was in a modern church hall situated in a residential area of the city of Birmingham, which takes pride in its promotion of cross-cultural activities.

My production was entitled *Hannya Miriam*. The principal performer was Nobushige Kawamura, a Noh actor of high reputation. Born into a famous Noh family, forty-one years of age, he is at the prime of a stage career that began when he was three years old. This means he is thoroughly immersed in the traditions of Shintoism, the indigenous religion of Japan with eight million deities, and Buddhism, whose ethos dominates most of the classical Noh dramas of his repertory. With the open attitude of a professional actor, this performer of mixed religious spirituality plays the role of a biblical figure, Miriam.

Before the production, I addressed the audience, sharing the background of this biblical Noh drama. I emphasized the necessity in the contemporary world to recognize our neighbour, though having a different religious heritage, as a loving partner. Loyalty to one's faith is compatible with the ability to respect other religious traditions. Hegemony of one religion over others was a mistake of the past, when the language of war overtook the language of love, even in the world of faith.

After the performance people asked many questions, including the question mentioned in the introduction. They enjoyed participating in a series of body movements. The whole audience stood up and became involved. Formality was broken and sense of communion prevailed. Raising a hand and pointing in the distance, as if pursuing Jesus, and spreading both hands wide apart, as if sharing with neighbours, the people enjoyed some basics of Noh performance with theological interpretation.

The future prospect. In November 1997 *Hannya Miriam* was played in a larger scale, on a historical Noh stage in Kyoto with a full orchestra of traditional musical instruments. Two more international performances of the same play are planned: in Bali in July 1998 at an Asian liturgical workshop, and in Harare in December 1998 at the fiftieth anniversary of the World Council of Churches.

The Hannya mask will be employed for these performances. I will share my reflection on Hannya, entitled *Through Anger God Speaks*. A selection is given here.

The word *hannya* is a Sanskrit word meaning true wisdom. Hannya refers to both a large collection of sutras and a short specific sutra made up with 262 ideograms. The Hannya Sutra (the Heart Sutra) is a prayer for salvation. The prayer originated with the Buddha and was written down later by his disciples. It is a popular sutra chanted throughout the world today.

The voice of the Hannya Sutra facilitates the salvation of the Noh character using a mask called Hannya.

The Noh mask Hannya is commonly identified as 'a female demon of jealousy and anger'. The naming is based on a hierarchical and androcentric projection and objectification, according to Josei shingaku (a Japanese feminist theology).

The demoniac feature is an expression of flaming rage and mortifying sorrow caused by injustice.

Her anger is a cry for wholeness.
Her wrath is a protest against objectification.
Her grimace is a prayer for healing.
By the cartharsis through Hannya's agony, people are healed.
Hannya transforms the values from negative into positive.
Hannya may be a form of God's love.

Conclusion

This article with its given title 'Performing Sacred Texts' started with a question, 'Why do you take all the trouble of writing, producing and showing the performance of biblical Noh dramas to people in and outside Japan?' My answer is the prophet Miriam's words, 'Has God spoken only through Moses? Has God not spoken through us also?' (Numbers 12.2).

Miriam, with full recognition of Moses' authority, advocates for a multivocal leadership. This challenge is a proof of Miriam's faith in God's creating each person, and in each individual's ability to respond to God's call. My answer comes from the same faith. God's word does not come only from the high ranking leaders, in a written and bounded canon of Hebrew, Greek, German or Anglo-Saxon languages. God also speaks to us in a non-verbal expression, such as dance and performing art.

The spontaneous performance of Miriam and Ameno Uzume is an important way of divine communication. It tends to be demeaned, because those in power fear the spontaneity. Inspired performances cannot be controlled, and anything that might undermine the present authority's controlling power tends to be oppressed, as history shows.

Performing arts have a power similar to that of sacraments. As Adams discerns, they heighten our concern for the material world. The dancing and the eating in worship make us aware of our material nature and hence our solidarity with and commitment to the world. Performing arts often reveal God as actively moving in us to help us identify ourselves with the dynamic God through our own movements. This is a direct fruit of performing sacred texts. We understand better the way God created us. We appreciate Jesus Christ becoming flesh. Knowing our physical limitation and potentiality by dancing, we realize the preciousness of sacraments, especially the eucharist. God allows us to eat and drink divine flesh and blood, enabling us to embody God's word.

Every child, woman and man embodies a sacred text. It is sacred because it is set apart specially for that person. All through one's life she/he performs the text, co-authored by God. Jesus is the choreographer/ coach/director who knows each one's talent and limitation, as well as potentiality. As every performer knows, when the basic skills of movement and voice are thoroughly mastered, one can perform to one's best without being conscious of each note or movement. Everyone can sing and dance naturally when in tune with the cosmic energy. When we discover our personal sacred text, the Holy Spirit works within us.

Performing sacred texts is fundamental to the feminist movement. It is a process of discovering the Bible in a non-biblical world (Kwok Pui-lan). The search for divine power in people's life is based on Masao Takenaka's biographical theology. The creation of biblical Noh drama is a stage version of story theology. (C. S. Song). Phyllis Trible points at the women's agony as the source of Hannya voice. Karen Lebacqz's analyses clarify the location and category of the agony. Katherine D. Sakenfeld's textual approach intensifies the biblical reading. The widened horizon of the theology of religions owes much to Yasuo Furuya. The perspective of Josei Shingaku was developed by Hisako Kinukawa. Chung Hyun-kyung inspires us with the declaration, 'we are the text'. Kim Yong Bock allows the thoughts of many Asian theologians, including Elizabeth Tapia, flowing into my Noh texts. Edna Orteza's dynamism enlarges the Noh drama into educational resources for the ecumenical theme of Justice, Peace and Integrity of the Creation. The connection between drama and daily life was encouraged by Victoria Rue. Performing sacred texts is a product of the wisdom of the body (Cynthia Winton-Henry). It is empowered by the communicative performances of Hideo Kanze and Nobushige Kawamura. Lee Hong Jung connected the community of church congregation and theological students with Noh drama. The reality of women, with the active exchange of members, particularly of Kamogawa-kai and Tasha (two cross-cultural groups that I founded in Kyoto for promoting respect of differences), continues to be the resourceful texts. Hideo Yuki contextualizes the texts in the Japanese cultures and religions. All these chains of network began with my encounter with a book that kindled in me a flame named the hermeneutics of suspicion (Elisabeth Schüssler Fiorenza). Respecting the process of formation of performing sacred texts, which is personal, communal and relational, I acknowledge these people in my journey of seeking feminist ways.

Selected bibliography

Adams Doug, and Diane Apostolos-Cappadona (eds.), *Dance as Religious Studies*, New York 1990.

Chung, Hyun Kyung, *Struggle to Be the Sun Again: Introducing Asian Women's Theology*, Maryknoll and London 1990.

Kim, Yong-Bock, *Messiah and Minjung: Christ's Solidarity with the People for New Life*, Hong Kong 1992.

Kinukawa, Hisako, *Women and Jesus in Mark: A Japanese Feminist Perspective*. Maryknoll 1994.

Kwok, Pui-lan, *Discovering the Bible in the Non-Biblical World*, Maryknoll 1995.

Schüssler Fiorenza, Elisabeth, *But She Said: Feminist Practices of Biblical Interpretation*, Boston 1992.

——, *In Memory of Her: A Feminist Theological Reconstruction of Christian Origins*, New York and London 1983.

Song, C. S., *Tell Us Our Names: Story Theology from an Asian Perspective*, Maryknoll 1984.

Trible, Phyllis, *Texts of Terror: Literary-feminist Readings of Biblical Narratives*, Philadelphia and London 1984.

Praxis-Exegesis: A Jewish Feminist Hermeneutic

Bonna Devora Haberman

Jewish tradition has continuously been preoccupied with the exposition of the relationship between religious text and action. The Torah, the Hebrew scripture, is itself studied as a source book for human spiritual, ethical, social, ritual and political life in the context of divine creation and revelation. According to mystical understandings, the Torah is even a guidebook for God's creation, God's action. While the Torah is the most rudimentary source for Jewish law, the ongoing human exegetical process expressed in rabbinic literature (which extends to this contemporary historical moment) is the method by which determinations are made about action. Rabbinic discourses often embellish, alter and sometimes even contradict biblical prescriptions where they are viewed as inappropriate or inapplicable. Though there is a pretence about the possibility of a 'simple' reading of the text, it is performed with acknowledgment of 'seventy faces to the Torah' which are understood to exist concurrently as multiple facets and layers of potential meanings. The biblical text is apprehended as the primary source for the halakhic system, the initial legal-literary-spiritual rubric. Ongoing discursive exegesis in rabbinic Judaism is the medium through which action in all of these realms is continuously negotiated with text.

In this article I propose a view of the relationship between text and action which conceives action as text interpretation proper. The praxis-exegete combines texts with intentional actions through the agency of exegesis. Attempting to convey the interpenetrability of text and human action, I undertake to erode the boundaries of the page which separate sacred texts from action. Culled from Jewish sources, this view has far-reaching implications both for exegesis and activisim in other traditions. Consider the following Talmudic passage about the relation between study and action.

> Rabbi Tarfon and the elders were reclining in the upper story of Nithza's house in Lod.
>
> The question was asked before them: 'Which is greater, study or action?'
>
> Rabbi Tarfon answered and said: 'Action is greater.'
>
> Rabbi Akiva answered and said: 'Study is greater.'
>
> Everyone answered and said: 'Study is greater because study leads to action' (bKiddushin 40b).

Rabbinic tradition considers the study and interpretation of holy texts to be valuable in its own right. The fulfilment of the biblical injunction to study is enigmatically equated in weight to all of the other commandments.[1] This passage from the Babylonian Talmud conveys an instrumental view of study: study has a causal connection with action. Study is the worthiest pursuit *because* it contributes to worthy action. The concluding statement which links study to action may only be comprehended in the light of the two previous opinions which assert the significance of each. Study achieves a relational primacy to action, from which it derives the utmost merit of action.

This Talmudic discussion is premised upon a network of tacit assumptions. The rabbis believe that it is possible and desirable to influence people's actions. Their aim is to encourage what they consider to be 'good' action. Both of these views express a prior assumption that action consists of more than behaviourally observable events or actions. Human consciousness wilfully fulfils intentions by causing observable actions. Intentions, according to the view proposed here, are unseen roots; actions are the trunk and branches.[2] Intentions inform, inspire or motivate human actions. In the Talmudic text, it is the actors' intentions which the rabbis understand to be influenced by study. As a result of learning Torah, claims the text, a human being is motivated to express her learning by performing her interpretation of the text through action. Her action thereby articulates her understanding of God's intentions about her life as they are revealed in the process of her engagement with sacred texts.

I need to clarify my positioning of this Jewish source. The attribution of authority to Talmudic discourse (in which I am tacitly partaking by citing the text) amplifies the relevance of the text beyond its co-ordinates in time and place. Within Jewish culture, textual exegesis does not simply express opinions; it participates in the holiness of God's ongoing revelation. The process of study, interpretation and actualization to which this text refers is contextually understood to be an enduring spiritual obligation to fulfil God's will, a process in which I am participating through this current exegesis. The declaration of the preferred value of study-which-leads-to-action, therefore, is reflexive: by prescribing the preference of study, the text boldly asserts its own pertinence to the reader who holds it in hand at the instant of studying it. The text addresses the reader about itself, advocating the legitimacy of its own claim on the life of the reader at the same instant as proposing its efficacy to alter/improve the reader's actions. The authority of this specific text, however, is tempered by its injunction to study and perpetuate the interpretative process. By the very assertion of the primacy of the conjoined activities of study and action, the text relegates itself to the status of contingency in an encompassing cycle of human agency. The text is an object of study, which occasions interpretations, which are fulfilled in actions. Rather than a dyad of text-action, this passage proposes a continuum of experience whereby texts are set into motion by intentional study. The question for the rabbis is not '*Text* or action?', but '*Study* or action?'; the answer is not study, but study-which-leads-to-action. I propose that the text is activated by the intention of the reader to interpret; the interpretation is accomplished not only in the medium of discourse, but, I am suggesting, through actions.

My reading of the Talmudic passage proposes that text and action are bound together in processes of intentional interpretation. Texts and actions are, nevertheless, different media of human experience. The clarification of the connection between text and action requires some discussion of distinctions and relevant similarities. If they are kept remote from one another, the text is inert on the shelf; the action vivacious, but uninformed by the volumes which contextualize it.

In much the same way as art is not sufficiently rendered by description or interpretation, so actions also are not sufficiently rendered by description or interpretation. Texts are apparently two-dimensional, actions three-dimensional. Actions cannot be reduced to print or canonized as text. Even ritual acts can never be reproduced with the same precision as text may be reprinted and photocopied. The human performers of actions, their feelings, their relationships, the context and combinations are endlessly variable, whereas the immutable precision of a text appears printed in black and white upon the page. Text, therefore, boasts an initial form which purports to be accessible. We can take the text in hand, scrutinize, compare and dissect it. It is fixed in form and content; reproducible. Whereas an action transpires once uniquely, on the page, even anachronistic utterances can transpire simultaneously: biblical Moses can enter the rabbinic study hall of Rabbi Akiva. Though the ink on the page of a text often feigns discontinuity from the subjective hand of the author, it is usually the product of her/his selective personal refinement and tedious editing.

Once an initial action has transpired, there is no means of access to the action itself; an action can be replayed or re-experienced only in memory. Accounts, descriptions and documentation of every kind are, by definition, *post factum* and removed. This 'irretrievability' of action appears to be in sharp contrast with the eminent reproducibility of text. The contrast, however, is dissolved by the common dependency of both action and text for meaning and significance upon the subjectivity of human interpret tion. We can no more retrieve the author's or redactor's original intention and meaning of a text than we can exactly reconstruct an action, its meaning and significance.

Having contrasted the two media, text and action, I re-emphasize my original connection between them. My analysis points to their meeting in human intentional agency. Texts and actions are both expressions of human intentions to interpret. Even the ascription of divinity to the revealed biblical text entails a human recorder-interpreter of God's words. Texts and actions are bound together by their shared cultural frameworks and systems of belief which render them meaningful. Both action and text are mediated by perceptions, selective memory, attitudes, preconceptions, concerns and intentions of reporters and exegetes. These mediating factors are relatively invisible or visible, depending upon the extent to which the actors, reporters and readers share the perspective(s) from which they view or experience both text and action and their subsequent descriptions and interpretations. One does not tend to notice the Christian bias of liberal rhetoric when one has been socialized in Western Christian culture. However, with eyes sensitized to the texts and experiences of a different religious tradition, the Christian assumptions are seen in sharp relief. Within most common cultural discourse, specific epistemological, religious and normative assumptions dominate. Taken together, these assumptions interact to form a matrix, a paradigm of dominant or hegemonic discourse. Hegemonic discourse is inextricable from those who wield institutional and political power in their cultural context. Indeed, it reflects the values and interests of those who dominate.

In Western cultural contexts. Elisabeth Schüssler Fiorenza has termed dominance by elite male, white Christians 'kyriarchy'.[3] Through control of the instruments of socialization and the manufacture of culture, kyriarchal assumptions are rendered invisible. By virtue of their invisiblity, dominant assumptions and their attendant interpretations perpetuate the power and authority of those who support and are supported by them. Invisibly, they convey moral and political preferences and biases which consistently favour and reinscribe the interests of the master empowered white male elite. In connection with her critical work on documentary film, Trinh Minh-Ha discusses her perception of the intractableness of the dominant assumptions, and the power of the interests that they remain invisible:

> It is as if the acknowledgment of the politics of the documentation and the documenting subject disturbs because the interests at stake are too high for the guardians of the norms.[4]

The desirability of revealing heretofore invisible assumptions, therefore, is directly related to the extent to which we perceive ourselves dissenting from them, being excluded, dominated or oppressed by them. Feminist scholars and theologians have extensively and cogently argued that systems of interpretation of religious texts and life are seamlessly participating in the domination and oppression of women. The androcentric veil which rendered gender bias invisible has been lifted.[5] The consequent visibility of kyriarchy within the canon itself and in the interpretative literatures and, I suggest, institutions and enactments has led to a spectrum of feminist responses. For some, it has completely shaken the possibility of faith; for others, it has led to minor and radical revisions. Feminist methods of expressing responses to misogyny perceived in sacred sources, reading against the grain, filling in gaps with new midrashic elaborations, creating alternative narratives, have proliferated.

I am proposing a method which builds upon the theological and practical inroads made by the recent generation of feminist scholars and activists. The proximity and mutual connection of text and action enables intentional engagement in interpretative praxis-exegesis. Normative behaviours, practices, rituals are inextricable from their textual referents, constantly interpreting and influencing the readings, affirming and re-inscribing kyriarchy, or potentially de-constructing and revisioning it. Media, text and action are all engaged with one another in cultural-political processes, conjoined by the inexorable subjectivity of interpretation.

I conceive an interconnected web of intentionally re-interpretative texts and actions, conjoined as 'praxis-exegesis'. One of my conscious intentions in proposing praxis-exegesis is to problematize and transform accepted interpretations by means of reinterpretative actions. Restrictions on women's roles in sacred traditions, access to textual knowledge, authority and concomitant leadership roles in public ritual may be challenged and undermined through praxis-exegesis. Women have the possibility to choose to enact their new interpretations of sacred texts and liturgies. Convening study groups to engage in the process of interpretation; generating new curricula and methods which empower praxis-exegesis in seminaries and institutes; initiating prayer groups to experiment with liturgical forms and choreographies; creating meetings to initiate authorities into praxis interpretations; mobilizing those disaffected by the kyriarchal bias of traditional reading and practice, are all examples of re-interpretations through praxis-exegesis.

The word 'praxis' derives from the Greek: doing, acting, action, practice. Karl Marx conceived of praxis as revolutionary change. Marx's claim that the enterprise of study, inquiry and theory about truth is inextricable from practice is germane to the view I express here. Study, according to Marx, has as its aim the proof and realization of its findings in the material realm of action.[6] For Marx, theory aims to motivate the will to act; the goal of knowledge is the reconfiguration of power. Though I share the liberationist aim, I depart from the narrowness of Marx's theoretical system of which his degradation of religion was a symptom. Alongside his sustained social critique, Marx professed a self-contradictory reductionism whereby the undoing of oppressive religion, epitomized by Judaism, was one of the tenets of his theory.[7]

Liberation theologians have specifically addressed this deficiency in Marx's thought by creating interpretations of religious life which aim to generate revolutionary praxis.[8] Liberation theology combines an axiomatic belief in religious tradition with an ethico-political commitment to freedom from oppression. Whereas oppressors use the biblical narratives to justify their domination, liberationists interpret the same texts to validate their faith that 'God gives people courage and power to resist dehumanization and slavery'.[9] Liberationist theologians seek the fulfilment of religious faith *through* liberationist praxis.[10] The liberationist claim that religious faith promotes and is affirmed by struggles for freedom is a possibility which Marx never entertained.

Until relatively recently, feminism accepted Marx's hypothesis about religion uncritically.[11] Feminists blamed biblical tradition for patriarchy, as Marx blamed religion for oppression. Meanwhile, religious feminists committed to their biblical traditions have begun to elaborate more sophisticated liberation theology positions whereby theology is conceived as a multi-disciplinary integration of human inquiry which is fulfilled through praxis.[12] These feminists see women as the paradigmatic object of oppression whose liberation is pivotal to the entire matrix of global transformation. The uniquely religious character of this evolving feminist discourse engages primarily with biblical texts: through critique, reinterpretation and 'reading against the grain'.[13] The praxis-exegetical method which I am proposing here not only advocates activism as an outcome of feminist reinterpretation; it conceives actions as a medium of interpretation. The realm of actions is connected by the intentionality of the interpreter to textual sources, biblical, rabbinic; Jewish and other. Praxis-exegesis, therefore, is a method of liberationist interpretation which interfuses the boundary of the page of text with the surrounding life context by means of the activity of the interpreter. Life actions are like the script forming layered margins of interpretation around a Talmudic page. This praxis-exegesis is not a linear process whereby prescriptive texts dictate corresponding actions according to fixed general principles or theories. I conceive praxis-exegesis as a web of intersecting texts and actions, connected by peoples' intentions to interpret. The task of the praxis-exegete is intentionally to constitute the realm of interpretation, recounting the chosen actions within a 'con-textuality', proposing contiguous texts, and to enact her interpretation textually and literally, so to speak, in action.

In December 1988, I convened a group of Israeli women from diverse backgrounds and affiliations for prayers in celebration of *Rosh Hodesh*, the new month, at the Western Wall. According to the practice of each, some wore fringed prayer shawls, the traditional garment of Jewish prayer. We brought with us a Torah scroll for the customary reading. We were physically assaulted, cursed and forced out of the Western Wall plaza by a mob of ultra-Orthodox women and men who burst through the partition which separates the genders. During a number of subsequent incidents, the violence escalated, while the police denied us protection, in spite of our efforts to secure a resolution through meetings with the responsible officials. We petitioned the Supreme Court of Israel, calling on the State to give cause why it had not protected our basic rights to religious freedom of practice and access to holy sites.[14] The Supreme Court process has been an arduous and continuous trail of widely interspersed hearings and rulings. At the same time as pursuing the legal-political struggle, Women of the Wall have persisted in convening monthly for *Rosh Hodesh*, a traditional women's celebration of the new month, at the Western Wall throughout this nine-year period.

Here is an exemplary text which I interpret to demonstrate the interactive hermeneutics of praxis-exegesis. In July 1989, Rabbi Mayer Yehuda Getz distributed these flyers to Women of the Wall as we entered the Western Wall plaza for *Rosh Hodesh* prayers. I cite the full text of the letter.

Rabbi Mayer Yehuda Getz,
In Charge of the Western Wall and Sacred Sites adjacent to the Temple Mount,
PO Box 14123,
Jerusalem, Israel   Rosh Hodesh Tammuz, 5749

Dear and Honoured Sister,
My sincerest blessings to you as you stand before the Western Wall, remnant of the holy temple; the most hallowed area for the nation of Israel to which we can come at the present time.

While standing here, it is incumbent on us all to recall the soldiers of Israel who shed their blood and lost their lives so that we can pray at the Western Wall in peace and tranquility.

With all my heart I ask you to help me in the difficult task of guarding the sanctity of this place. Do not stray from the hallowed traditions of generations of Jews before you who have mourned here for Zion; Zion which the Almighty has granted us in our time.

I extend to you the blessing which Eli the High Priest bestowed upon Chana, mother-to-be of Samuel the Prophet.

> May the God of Israel grant your petition which you plead from Him (I Samuel 1.17).

Come in peace and return in peace, and may the Almighty answer all our prayers for peace in our land, for the nation of Israel and for the entire world.

Respectfully,
Rabbi Mayer Yehuda Getz

Rabbi Getz's text demanded the attention of Women of the Wall by virtue of his authority as the appointee of the Ministry of Religious Affairs responsible for the Western Wall. As Women of the Wall entered the holy space to pray, we were expected to superimpose his page of text on top of our prayer books, place it in the front of our consciousness. Rabbi Getz, we know, was the father of two sons who were killed liberating the wall from Jordanian authority during the 1967 war. He writes to us vividly of their blood and death in contrast to the peace and tranquility to which he aspires. He implores us to mourn for them as he does. His blessing for Women of the Wall is the one addressed to Hannah. Rabbi Getz asserts the relevance of the biblical text from I Samuel to the contemporary actions of Women of the Wall. He identifies himself with Eli, the High Priest, the guardian of a Jewish holy space (I Samuel 1). The identification of Rabbi Getz with Eli is enigmatic: Eli had gravely misinterpreted Hannah and mistaken her for a mumbling drunkard. Once Eli recognizes the sincerity of Hannah's supplication, his blessing is that God grant Hannah's prayer. Rabbi Getz qualifies the blessing that our prayers should be fulfilled; he asserts the primacy of the petition for peace. His tacit assumption is that Women of the Wall caused the disruption of peace, or at least have the power to promote peace. If only we would behave!

Hannah's-Women of the Wall's experience of Eli's-Rabbi Getz's degrading misinterpretation of our prayer screams from the page in hand. Hannah is not disciplined by Eli in the Samuel text; she is given the opportunity to explain her cause. Having listened to Hannah's own words, Eli reverses his judgmental reproach, and responds with the blessing which Rabbi Getz cites. Whereas Hannah establishes the paradigm of prayer, according to rabbinic tradition,[15] Women of the Wall are admonished without the opportunity to speak. Hannah had prayed initially in her heart, with only her lips moving. Rabbi Getz implies that this is how women should pray; and has explicitly stated this opinion in conversation. The finale of the biblical source, Hannah's prayer recorded in the second chapter of I Samuel, contradicts Rabbi Getz's aim. Though its authenticity as a women's song is debated by scholars, the fact of its appearance in the redacted narrative emphasizes the audibility and, therefore, legibility of her text.

The reinterpretative praxis-exegesis which the prayer-action by Women of the Wall articulate problematizes Rabbi Getz's text. Instead of appealing to a source which will convince us to comply and be silenced, Women of the Wall highlight the incongruity between his biblical proof text and subsequent rabbinic tradition which records and affirms Hannah's prayer; and the fact that contemporary women are silenced. Women of the Wall's claims are strengthened by the analogy to Hannah; Rabbi Getz is indicted for re-enacting Eli's misinterpretation of women's prayer. I read a poignant irony in the juxtaposition of Rabbi Getz's statement 'Do not stray from the hallowed traditions of generations of Jews before you who have mourned here for Zion', with 'Zion which the Almighty has granted us in our time'. But does not the 'tradition' of silencing women which he advocates stray from his textual source? We are also aware of how long Zion has mourned *because* the Temple site was inaccessible. The cause for mourning was inaccessibility. Now, admits Getz, the Almighty has granted the petition to return to Jerusalem the holy city. Therefore, Women of the Wall approach the wall no longer in mourning, though we mourn the cost of dear life which was lost in war. Our consciousness is not directed backwards to replicate the mourning prayer of exiles. Hannah's song marks the fulfilment of her supplication; Women of the Wall's celebration marks the homecoming not only of the Jewish people, but of women to the public holy domain. Whereas Hannah's petition was personal and individual, Women of the Wall assert a symbolic public vision of homecoming for the Jewish people.

Homecoming is action. It involves movement towards a defined material space and the work, sometimes blood, of material transformation. It requires reinterpretation of the former relationships of exile, otherwise, even at home, we experience life in exile. Praxis is an intentional combining of these two components. Through praxis, exile is transformed into the 'beginning of the flowering of our redemption'.[16]

The actions by which Women of the Wall deconstructed and reinterpreted Rabbi Getz's letter are an example of praxis-exegesis. The extensive documentation of Women of the Wall, from which this letter is an excerpt, records the events, arguments and decisions about a feminist challenge to state and religious institutions and structures of kyriarchal authority. Rabbi Getz's letter was later reproduced in the State's 270-page response to our 1989 Supreme Court petition, encoded not only in the exchange of specific women with a state authority, but in the Israeli government's self-justification to the Supreme Court for new legislation.[17] The persistent prayer-actions of the women are etching new images and visions into sacred stone pages.

The praxis-exegesis which I propose here is rooted in a Talmudic view about the motivation of action by study. I conceive *praxis* as a public hermeneutic activity of intentional interpretation through both media of text *and* action. Actions become praxis when they are conjoined with the intention to interpret, either by the actor(s), or, in the absence of the actors' intention, by another person. Action, according to this view, is an interpretative medium. The coupling of interpretative intention with actions is praxis-exegesis. Intention without action is insufficient for praxis-exegesis. This view refines and bolsters the rabbis' study-generates-action.

I exhort the interpretative community not only to be attentive to praxis-exegesis, but also to create strategies and initiate it. Feminist liberation theologians sound a call to action based on the connection between spirituality and politics.[18] Religion, following the prophetic tradition, must become an effective agent of change toward a more just world. Your hands which grip the text for the purpose of reading have the possibility of praxis-exegesis: intentionally to interpret through actions which reach beyond the boundary of the page.

Notes

1. Mishnah Peah 1.1.

2. Cf. bKiddushin 40b.

3. *Jesus: Miriam's Child, Sophia's Prophet: Critical Issues in Feminist Christology*, New York and London 1994, 12–18; Rosemary Radford Ruether, *Sexism and God-Talk: Towards a Feminist Theology*, Boston and London 1983, 72–82, 93–99.

4. Trinh Minh-Ha, *Framer Framed*, New York and London 1992, 119.

5. Carol Christ, 'Toward a Paradigm Shift in the Academy and in Religious Studies', in *The Impact of Feminist Research in the Academy*, ed. Christie Farnham, Indiana 1987, 54.

6. 'The German Ideology' (1845–6), *Karl Marx Selected Writings*, ed. D. McLellan, Oxford 1977, 156.

7. Amy Newman argues that Marx even participated in the antisemitic discourse about ritual murder in his effort to discredit religion, 'Feminist Social Criticism and Marx's Theory of Religion', *Hypatia* 9 (4), 1994, 15–37.

8. Gustavo Gutiérrez, a Peruvian, wrote one of the early systematic accounts of liberation theology: *A Theology of Liberation*, Maryknoll and London 1973, [2]1988.

9. J. H. Cone, 'Christian Faith and Political Praxis', in B. Mahan and L. D. Dale (eds.), *The Challenge of Liberation Theology: A First World Response*, Maryknoll 1981, 59.

10. Marsha Aileen Hewitt, *From Theology to Social Theory. Juan Luis Segundo and the Theology of Liberation*, New York 1990.

11. See Amy Newman's 'Feminist Social Criticism' (n. 7).

12. Rosemary Radford Ruether, *Liberation Theology. Human Hope Confronts Christian History and American Power*, New York 1972; Mary Daly, *Beyond God the Father. Toward a Philosophy of Women's Liberation*, Boston and New York 1973.

13. See Phyllis Trible, *Texts of Terror*, Philadelphia 1984.

14. Israeli Supreme Court Appeal: *Bagatz 257/89*.

15. bBerakhot 31a-b.

16. From the text of the Israeli Chief Rabbinate's prayer for the Welfare of the State of Israel.

17. *Bagatz 257/89*.

18. Judith Plaskow, 'Feminist Judaism and Repair of the World', in Carol J. Adams (ed.), *Ecofeminism and the Sacred*, New York 1993, 70–1.

III · Concluding Reflection

Reflection on Women's Sacred Scriptures

Kwok Pui-lan

Coming from diverse social and cultural backgrounds, the contributors to this *Concilium* issue have powerfully argued that the notions of scripture, canon, authority and interpretation need to be radically reconceptualized, based on women's experiences from different parts of the world. First, the concept of scripture as understood by the West has derived from the Bible. This culturally-specific understanding is too narrow to encompass the multiscriptural traditions of world religions and women's diverse experiences. Second, women's voices and stories have been largely left out of the established canons of the historical religions of humankind. Using the hermeneutics of suspicion, women from different cultures and religions have posed significant challenges to the boundaries of canon and authority of the written word. Third, the Bible and other sacred writings have been used as ideological tools to justify slavery, colonization, cultural hegemony, genocide and patriarchal domination. A post-colonial reading of sacred texts opens new avenues to explore the intersection between truth, knowledge and power. Fourth, feminist scholars have expanded the notion of scripture to include many non-written forms. In addition to critical feminist literary studies, there is the need to develop new hermeneutical tools to interpret oracles, performances, dances and exegesis-actions.

What is sacred scripture?

Many feminist scholars have pointed out that women's experiences have largely been left out or insufficiently reflected in the sacred texts of the historical religions. But several contributors have emphasized that women have not been passive recipients of sacred scriptures. Rather, they have actively participated in the reconstruction of sacred texts and expanded their traditional boundaries. In her provocative article, Elsa Tamez urges us to see a woman's body as sacred text: 'Women's bodies, then, can manifest themselves as sacred text setting out their stories to be read and re-read and to generate liberating actions and attitudes. Women's lives enshrine a deep grammar, whose morphology and syntax need to be learned for the sake of better human inter-relationships' (p. 63). In her semiotic juxtaposition of the body of women and the body of the text, Tamez challenges any reified notion of scripture as something bound, closed and handed down from a bygone era. Instead of relegating women's experiences to the periphery of holy scripture, she places women's lives at the centre of a construction of 'text' that is living, pluralistic and multi- stranded. Speaking from the Latin American context, Tamez argues that women's bodies bear witness to systemic violence and discrimination, as well as to the continual struggle for survival and well-being. God did not speak in the past only, because whenever women fight for their dignity and freedom, there is the epiphany of God. There is the new text. Tamez suggests that women as a living text must be read intratextually with the religious texts.

Echoing Tamez, Joan Martin, an African American ethicist, expands the notion of sacred text to include the slave narrative. The slave narratives are a rich depository of the memories, stories, hopes and fears of enslaved women and men under the extremely dehumanizing conditions of chattel slavery. The slave narratives of blackwomen, in particular, point to their subjective understanding of womanhood, their relationship to God, and their daily struggles as moral agents. Martin gives several reasons why the slave narratives should be considered sacred text. These narratives are a collective narration of a significant event that united and shaped the identity of the African American community. Just as the Exodus story is told and re-told because it is foundational to the Jewish identity, the slave narratives are collective narrations which give African American people a sense of where they came from and where they are going. The slave narratives are sacred also because they bear witness to the power of the Spirit. 'It is in this collective experiential nature of the narrative – oral and written, in expressing faith journeys, clandestine worship, fervent prayer, and ultimate hopes lifted to God – that the slave narrative approaches "sacred text"' (p. 70). Slave narratives provide primary data of enslaved people's humanity and religion. They are sacred sources for the construction of womanist ethics and theology, although Martin does not claim that they have the same stature as the Bible.

Other contributors who discuss more directly the relationship between women and traditional religious texts point to women's agency in selection, interpretation and transposition of scripture. Ivonne Gebara elucidates how women's relationship with scripture varies according to class, social status and educational background. Women's responses to sacred scripture are multivocal and cannot be easily generalized. Her work with poor and uneducated women in Brazil indicates how these women have discovered authority in themselves, rather than depending on an outside authority, through the process of conscientization. The Bible becomes an ally in their struggles as they learn to relate the texts to their present needs and reject the imposed authority of the church and religious hierarchy. Gebara criticizes male Latin American theologians for failing to come to grips with the androcentrism of the biblical text and religious leadership. Their failure to understand human liberation in gendered terms hinders them from acknowledging androcentric elements in the Bible and women's ambivalent attitudes toward the text.

In a totally different context, Yuko Yuasa defies traditional canonical boundary by bringing the story of the Ameno Uzume in Japan into dialogue with the story of Miriam in the Bible. In Japan's pluralistic religious society where people often have more than one religious identity, such transposition of religious texts may be more acceptable than in the West. Yuasa is a pioneer who creates and directs biblical Noh drama, an ancient and stylistic tradition many centuries old. Her attempt points to the important performative dimension of scripture in Hindu, Shinto and Buddhist traditions. Furthermore, the performance of biblical drama is not simply an exercise of interpretation. It is a re-creation or re-constitution of the text based on present circumstances and the needs of audiences. In less rigid and stylistic performances, the artists and storytellers can often improvise according to the responses of the audiences. Thus, the audiences also participate in the re-writing of the text.

In these several examples, we have seen that a notion of the scripture as fixed, bound and written, containing the sole revelation of God, is foreign to the religious experiences of women in many cultural contexts. While those at the centre of power tend to hold on to authoritative claims of sacred texts to justify the *status quo*, many women at the margin have deconstructed such claims and located sacredness in their own bodies, lives, foundational stories, myths and legends. Their relationship with sacred text is no longer obedience and submission, but active reconceptualization, creative performance and courageous proclamation. Scripture is no longer a dead cultural or religious artefact, but a living continuous *process*.

The erasure of women's words

Several contributors discuss the processes by which women's words were systematically erased from the canon of sacred texts. Investigating the process by which the Bible changed from an oral tradition to a written text, Joanna Dewey's work has argued that women's words were either left out or presented in a skewed written form controlled by the male literate elites. Comparing oral authority with manuscript-based authority, she says that the former is 'inherently democratic or egalitarian' and the latter tends to be more elitist. While this generally holds true, I would like to see more cross-cultural studies and comparison. For in some oral cultures, men still have more authority than women to speak. In Islam and Hinduism, great importance has been attached to the oral transmission of the scripture, but women have not had the same access to authority.

While Dewey examines how Christianity began with the 'discipleship of equals' and ended with the subordination of women in the first centuries through tracing the development from oral stories to written text, S. N. A. Parratt presents a fascinating contemporary case in which the authority of women was usurped in Meitei religion. In this tradition, the spoken liturgy and proclamation of oracles are the central forms of 'scripture'. These oracles come from the goddess to the priestesses, who play a pre-eminent role in the tradition. The attempt of male priests to record the oracles in written form and to canonize them takes away the religious authority of women. Parratt attributes this patriarchal take-over to the influences of Hinduism, which disavows women's religious leadership. But a larger question is how women's authority changes when oral cultures give way or partly change to the written culture. Other cases in Africa, Asia and other places can illuminate this particular issue.

Both Dewey and Karen King analyse the ways women's stories and writings are left out in the canonization process of the Bible. The Pastoral Epistles, which exhort women to remain in silence and submission, are included in the canon, Dewey points out, while the stories of Thecla, a female teacher and miracle worker were left out. King's historical study traces the transfiguration of Mary Magdala from a faithful apostle of Jesus to a lustful prostitute by early church fathers to fit the patriarchal ideology in the early centuries. The Gospel of Mary portrays her as Jesus' most beloved disciple, and the one Jesus selected to be given a special revelation. For King, the Gospel of Mary 'presents the clearest argument for the legitimacy of women's authority and leadership in early Christianity' (p. 33). But the Gospel of Mary was not included in the canon, and Mary was nowhere to be found in the Acts of Apostles. In contrast, other Gospels in which the male disciples feature prominently are included in the canon.

In the Islamic tradition, Amina Wadud points out, women's voices have been minimized in the canon. This is highly problematic for Muslim women, given the fact that the Qur'an has such critical importance in all aspects of life. Using her own personal experiences, Wadud demonstrates that men cannot interpret the Qur'an for women, who must search for and interpret the female voice of the text, so that a fuller and more comprehensive understanding can be achieved. I find her discussion of the female voice of Allah iconoclastic and hope to hear more from her how this female voice can be retrieved, given the centuries of the monopoly of male scholarship. I agree fully with M. W. Dube-Shomanah when she says that there is a dire need for feminist re-writing of sacred texts from the Third World and from traditions other than Christianity. While we have more than three decades of feminist scholarship on the Bible, feminist studies of other religious texts are only just beginning to emerge. Such discrepancy marginalizes the significance of other sacred texts and reinforces the centrality of feminist hermeneutics based on the Bible.

Even though women's voices are marginalized and left out in canonical texts, these scholars have suggested strategies to trace their hidden words. 1. Instead of accepting the existing canon, King argues that we should problematize 'the canon as a starting point for both historical reconstruction and theological reflection' (p. 34). 2. Both Dewey and King use extra-canonical materials, such as the Acts of Thecla and the Gospel of Mary. 3. Dewey encourages us to read against the grain. For example, instead of accepting the injunctions of the Pastoral Epistles that women be silent, we have to imagine that women were actually speaking and exercising their leadership. 4. Wadud suggests we actively imagine God's female voice and accent in the stories of women in the texts, such as the Queen of Sheba and Mary, the mother of Jesus. 5. We can re-write the script and re-cast the biblical drama, giving women more active roles, as Yuasa has hinted.

A post-colonial interpretation of the Bible

In her article, Dube-Shomanah raises the complex issues of interpreting the Bible from feminist and post-colonial perspectives. In the past two decades, post-colonial theories have offered new tools for analysing the text, contrapuntal reading strategies, and fresh ways of looking at power and knowledge. The works of Edward Said, Gayatri Chakravorty Spivak and Homi Bhabha are used and cited in multidisciplinary fields. Biblical scholars and theologians are just beginning to engage this body of literature to look at the Bible, hermeneutics and theological construction.

The discussion of post-colonial interpretation of the Bible has gained momentum among Third World scholars and intellectuals within the diasporic communities. R. S. Sugirtharajah has said that the post-colonial perspective has to go beyond a mimicry of Western interpretative methods and an Orientalist valorization of ancient pre-colonial cultures. It has to negotiate a different past, which was not reified, glorified and unitary. Employing tools from critical theory, literary and cultural studies, post-colonial criticism challenges both imperialist and nationalist claims, the silencing of subaltern and especially women, and maintains the posture of 'resistance literature'.

There are several characteristics of post-colonial criticism: 1. it challenges the totalizing forms of Western interpretation, exposing its co-optation by imperial interests and destabilizing its frame of meaning; 2. it is a counter-hegemonic discourse, paying special attention to the hidden and neglected voices in the Bible; 3. it places the Bible or any particular religious text within the multi-scriptural contexts of diverse settings; 4. it encourages and welcomes contributions from marginalized groups that have been neglected: the dalits, the indigenous peoples, the migrants, people in diaspora and in borderland, and especially women in these communities; and 5. it learns from and debates with other hermeneutical frameworks, such as poststructuralism and postmodernism.

Since the West had more contacts with Asia as a result of the discovery of sea-routes, expansion of trade and later colonization, people in the West had been fascinated with its ancient civilization, culture, and sacred texts. The East has sometimes been a romantic puzzle to the West. There is a tendency in the West to escape from its current ills and to find solace in unrealistic and imaginary worlds, a desire and longing for something that is timeless. On the other hand, there is the whole mechanism, which Edward Said describes in *Orientalism*, of constituting the Oriental subject for purposes of control and domination. The West's relationship with the East is full of unsettling tensions: of desire and longing as well as condemnation and control.

The encounter with the religious systems and sacred texts of Asia forced Western people, and especially the intellectuals, to re-examine their cultural identity and past heritage. The Western academic world was confronted with the fact that the Bible was not the only sacred text, when other manuscripts and religious texts were brought back to the metropolitan centres from the colonies and other places. The nineteenth century saw unprecedented interest in the study of comparative mythology, comparative philology, and sacred books from the East. The historical-critical method emerged in such a matrix when the West had to redefine itself and to re-assert its cultural superiority over the rapidly expanding colonized world. Ernest Renan, the author of the influential *La Vie de Jésus*, was a Phoenician archaeologist, comparative philologist, and a teacher of Oriental languages. He displayed deep-seated ethnocentric attitudes when comparing Semitic culture with European culture. The

German intellectual Leopold von Ranke, whose ideas influenced the historicism of the critical study of the Bible, referred to Eastern civilizations as 'nations of eternal standstill'. The historical-critical method was not a scientific, value-neutral discipline, as is often claimed, but was heavily clouded by the ethnocentric conceptualization of the West and the biblical interests of the imperialistic era.

Reading the development of the historical-critical method in a global framework leads me to ask questions about the power dynamics which caused one culturally-specific reading method to become the reigning paradigm in the academy for a long time. It is true that we have more reading paradigms today, such as rhetorical criticism, feminist criticism, cultural criticism, literary criticism, sociological criticism and reader response criticism. The assumptions and methodological underpinnings of these paradigms need to be scrutinized in multi-cultural and global perspectives to discern their usefulness for people who are struggling to read their religious texts for liberation.

I welcome Dube-Shomanah's contribution to the dialogue by raising specific questions regarding the intersection between feminism and post-colonial contexts. She convincingly argues that colonial powers have used Western canonical texts – both secular and religious – to colonize people. The question we need to ask further is whether this process of colonization of the mind is the same for women and men, as the colonized are gendered subjects. Furthermore, how did the propagation of other sacred texts affect the lives and circumstances of women? For example, the spread of the Qur'an and the loss of female voice was highlighted in Wadud's article. Parratt also mentions the influence of Hinduism on the Meitei tradition, which used to accord women significant religious roles. A cross-cultural comparison of the misuse of sacred scriptures to control women's power and voice will be very helpful.

Dube-Shomanah identifies commonalities and differences in feminist and post-colonial reading strategies. Both groups have to struggle against a canon that marginalizes them, derogatory images that legitimize their oppression, and hierarchical religious structures. But there are also different concerns and strategies as well. In particular, she urges Western feminist scholars and critics to regard the Bible as 'both patriarchal and *colonizing sacred canon*'. This is an important challenge which requires much self-critique and basic re-orientation.

Dube-Shomanah's research on the stories of the Syro-Phoenician woman and the Samaritan woman has led her to question the relation between biblical text and empire-building. She analyses the hidden interests, travel, geographical space and expansion in the stories of Jesus' journeying into foreign land. She points out that these texts have often legitimized the subjugation of foreign lands and people. She challenges Western feminists, saying that they have often highlighted the role of women in these stories without questioning the larger power dynamics involved. She writes: 'Seeking to restore women to biblical scriptures, and showing that women were active participants in the spread of the early church, is a strategy that did not problematize the ideology of the Christian misson or try to re-imagine the mission' (pp. 51f.). For Dube-Shomanah, it is not enough to focus on the sex/gender dimension of the text without simultaneously examining the multiple signification process embedded in it. She also urges Western feminists to read the biblical texts in the multi-faith situations of the world, not limiting the scope to the ancient Mediterranean world.

For many post-colonial subjects, interpretation of sacred texts is not simply an academic exercise, for action and reflection must be closely related. The final article by Bonna Devora Haberman gives a concrete example of how religious texts have been used by religious and political authorities to oppress women. In their decade-long struggle for the rights to holy sites, Women of the Wall used praxis-exegesis against the dogmatic and rigid interpretations by Rabbi Mayer. Haberman conceives action as text interpretation proper. 'The praxis-exegete combines texts with intentional actions through the agency of exegesis' (p. 91). Like other authors I have discussed, she wants to erode the boundaries between texts, bodies and action.

This collection of articles testifies to the multivocal and pluralistic relationships of women with sacred texts. Together they point to women's active reconceptualization of holy scripture and their unceasing quest for interpretation paradigms beyond androcentric and oppressive methods. I hope that feminist scholars who work on the Buddhist, Confucian and other indigenous traditions will join the cross-cultural dialogue in the future.

Suggested readings

Clarke, J.J., *Oriental Enlightenment: The Encounter between Asian and Western Thought*, London and New York 1997.

Donaldson, Laura E. (ed.), 'Postcolonialism and Scriptural Reading', *Semeia* 75, 1996, whole issue.

Kwok, Pui-lan, 'Jesus/the Native: Biblical Studies from a Postcolonial Perspective', in *Teaching the Bible: Discourses and Politics of Biblical Pedagogy*, ed. Segovia F. Fernando and Mary Ann Tolbert (forthcoming).

Sugirtharajah, R. S., 'From Orientalist to Post-Colonial: Notes on Reading Practice', *Asia Journal of Theology* 10, 1996, 20–7.

Contributors

IVONE GEBARA, a Sister of the Congregation of Sisters of Our Lady, teaches philosophy and theology. She is a member of and teacher for CESEP (Ecumenical Service Centre for Popular Education), a member of NEMGE (Centre for Studies in Women and Gender Questions) at the University of Sao Paulo, and a researcher for CNPQ (National Council for Scientific and Technological Development). She is co-author with Maria Clara Bingemer of *Mary: Mother of God and Mother of the Poor* (Eng. trans. 1993) and her other books include *Trindade – coisas velhas e novas* (1994), *Teologia em ritmo de mulher* (1994), and *Teologia ecofeminista* (1997).

Address: Rua Luiz Jorge dos Santos, 278, Tabatinga, 54756–380 Camaragibe – PE, Brazil.

JOANNA DEWEY is Associate Professor of New Testament Studies at the Episcopal Divinity School in Cambridge, MA. She received her PhD from the Graduate Theological Union in Berkeley, CA. She has taught at Oklahoma State University, Phillips Graduate Seminary in Enid, OK, and Colgate Rochester Divinity School, Rochester, NY. Her publications include *Markan Public Debate: Literary Technique. Concentric Structure and Theology in Mark 2:1–3:6*, SBLDS 48, Chico, CA 1980; *Orality and Textuality in Early Christian Literature*, Semeia 65, 1994 (ed.); the commentary on Mark in *Searching the Scriptures: A Feminist-Ecumenical Commentary*, ed. Elisabeth Schüssler Fiorenza, New York and London 1994, 2,470–509; and '1 Timothy', '2 Timothy', 'Titus' in *The Women's Bible Commentary*, Louisville 1992, 353–61, together with numerous articles on Mark. She also performs 'Women on the Way: A Feminist Retelling of Mark'.

Address: Episcopal Divinity School, 99 Brattle Street, Cambridge, MA 02138, USA.

KAREN L. KING is Professor of New Testament Studies and the History of Ancient Christianity at the Divinity School, Harvard University. Her areas of research in the history of ancient Christianity focus on Nag Hammadi and Gnosticism. She has written a number of articles on Mary Magdalene and the Gospel of Mary. She is the author of *Revelation of the Unknowable God with Text, Translation, and Notes to NHC IX,3 Allogenes*, Sonoma, Ca., 1995, and editor of *Images of the Feminine in Gnosticism*, Philadelphia, 1988, and *Women and Goddess Traditions*, Minneapolis 1997.

Address: Harvard University, The Divinity School, 45 Francis Avenue, Cambridge, Mass. 02138, USA.

AMINA WADUD is Assistant Professor in the Department of Philosophy and Religious Studies at Virginia Commonwealth University in Richmond. Her major area of research is Islam and Gender with a primary focus on alternative interpretation of the holy book, al-Qur'an. Although she is best known internationally for her scholarly contributions and in particular for her book *Qur'an and Woman*, she is also a human rights activist and the mother of five children. She spent 1997–1998 as a research associate in the Women's Studies Program at Harvard Divinity School and visiting lecturer in History of Religion.

Address: Virginia Commonwealth University, Dept of Philosophy and Religious Studies, Richmond, USA.

MUSA W. DUBE SHOMANAH is a New Testament Lecturer in the Department of Theology and Religious Studies, University of Botswana. She is the author of 'Readings of Semoya: Botswana Women's Interpretations of Matt. 15:21–28', in *Semeia* 73, Atlanta 1996, 111–29.

Address: University of Botswana, Department of Theology and Religious Studies, Private Bag 0022, Gaborone, Botswana.

ELSA TAMEZ was born in Mexico in 1950 and is currently Rector of the Latin American Biblical University in San José, Costa Rica. She holds degrees in theology, literature and linguistics from Costa Rica and a doctorate in theology from the University of Lausanne. She has been a member of the Ecumenical Theological Education committee of the WCC and a moderator of EATWOT. She has published articles on Quetzalcoatl and the Christian God, the utopic argument of Ecclesiasticus, justice and justification, and other subjects; she has edited books on 'Capitalism, Violence and Anti-Life', 'Liberation Theologians Speak about Women', 'The Feminine Face of Theology', translated into English as *Through Her*

Eyes (1989), and 'Women Take the Word'; her own books include a *Concise Spanish-Greek Dictionary*, and *The Bible of the Oppressed* (1982).

Address: Universidad Bíblica Latinoamericana, Calle 3, Avenidas 14 y 16, Apdo. 901–1000, San José, Costa Rica.

JOAN M. MARTIN is Associate Professor of Christian Social Ethics at Episcopal Divinity School, Cambridge, MA. An ordained Presbyterian minister, she has advocated gender, racial and economic justice as a pastor, an ecumenical executive, and a university chaplain prior to completing the PhD from Temple University in 1996. She has published essays and sermons, and is currently completing a book on the work ethic of nineteenth-century enslaved women. Her professional associations include immediate past co-chairperson, steering committee of the Women and Religion Section, American Academy of Religion.

Address: Episcopal Divinity School, Dept of Christian Social Ethics, Cambridge MA, USA.

SAROJ NALINI ARAMBAM PARRATT was born in Imphal, Manipur, India, and studied in Calcutta and London before gaining her PhD at Australian National University. She is currently Senior Lecturer in World Religions, University of Botswana. Her main publications are: *The Religion of Manipur*, Calcutta 1980; *Queen Empress vs Tikendrajit: the Anglo-Manipuri Conflict of 1891* (co-author); *The Pleasing of the Gods; Meitei Lai Haraoba* (co-author); she has also written numerous articles on religion and women's issues in India and southern Africa.

Address: Department of Theology and Religious Studies, University of Botswana, Private Bag 0022, Gabarone, Botswana.

YUKO YUASA trained at the Graduate School of Theology, Doshisha and San Francisco, and is a writer/research scholar at the Yugen Institute of Noh Studies in Kyoto. The biblical Noh dramas she has created have been staged in Japan and England. She leads cross-cultural communities with feminist principles.

Address: 61 Nakagawara, Shimogamo, Sakyo, Kyoto, Japan 606.

BONNA DEVORA HABERMAN was born in Ottawa, Canada, and has studied, taught and lectured in the United States, England and Israel. She received her PhD in philosophy and education from the University of London in

1986. In Jerusalem, she initiated and sustained a decade-long social change movement for women's religious rights at the Western Wall. She is currently a visiting scholar at the Harvard Divinity School, where she was a Research Associate and Visiting Lecturer in 1996–97. Her recent publications include: 'Women of the Wall: From Text to Praxis', *Journal of Feminist Studies in Religion* 13(1), 1997, 243–57; 'The Yom Kippur Avoda within the Female Enclosure', in Judith Kates and Gall Reimer (eds.), *Beginning Anew: A Woman's Companion to the High Holy Days*, New York 1997, 243–57.

Address: The Divinity School, Harvard University, 45 Francis Avenue, Cambridge, Mass. 02138, USA.

KWOK PUI-LAN received her doctorate from Harvard University and teaches theology at Episcopal Divinity School in Cambridge, Massachusetts. She has lectured on Asian feminist theology in many parts of the world. She is the author of *Chinese Women and Christianity, 1860–1927*, and co-editor of *Inheriting Our Mothers' Gardens: Feminist Theology in Third World Perspective*. Her articles also appear in *Semeia, Concilium* and the *East Asian Journal of Theology*.

Address: 99 Brattle Street, Cambridge, MA 02138, USA.

The editors wish to thank the great number of colleagues who contributed in a most helpful way to the final project for this issue.

M. Pilar Aquino	San Diego	USA
R. Aguirre	Bilbao	Spain
W. Bassett	San Francisco	USA
P. F. Carneiro de Andrade	S. Jôao del Rei MG	Brazil
J. R. Chandran	Bangalore	India
K. Derksen	Utrecht	Netherlands
F. Elizondo	Madrid	Spain
V. Elizondo	San Antonio, Texas	USA
I. Fischer	Graz	Austria
D. A. González-Montes	Salamanca	Spain
E. Green	Bari	Italy
M. Grey	Salisbury	England
H. Häring	Nijmegen	Netherlands
M. E. Hunt	Tübingen	Germany
W. G. Jeanrond	Lund	Sweden
A. Jensen	Tübingen	Germany
J. D. Magonet	London	England
M. J. Mananzan	Manila	Philippines
S. Marcos	Cuernavaca	Mexico
N. Mette	Münster	Germany
H. Meyer-Wilmes	Nijmegen	Netherlands
R. Page	Edinburgh	Scotland
A. Pieris	Gonawala-Kelaniya	Sri Lanka
J. Riches	San José	Costa Rica
D. Singles	Lyons	France
S. W. Sykes	Cambridge	England
C. Theobald	Paris	France
E. Wainwright	Banyo	Australia
J. T. Walsh	Gaborone	Botswana
F. Wilfred	Chepauk-Madras	India

Members of the Board of Directors

Foundation

Anton van den Boogard	President	Nijmegen	The Netherlands
Paul Brand	Secretary	Ankeveen	The Netherlands
Werner Jeanrond		Lund	Sweden
Dietmar Mieth		Tübingen	Germany
Christoph Theobald SJ		Paris	France
Miklós Tomka		Budapest	Hungary

Founders

Anton van den Boogaard	Nijmegen	The Netherlands
Paul Brand	Ankeveen	The Netherlands
Yves Congar OP†	Paris	France
Hans Küng	Tübingen	Germany
Johann Baptist Metz	Vienna	Austria
Karl Rahner SJ†	Innsbruck	Austria
Edward Schillebeeckx OP	Nijmegen	The Netherlands

Directors-Counsellors

José Oscar Beozzo	São Paolo, SP	Brazil
Virgil Elizondo	San Antonio, TX	USA
Seán Freyne	Dublin	Ireland
Hermann Häring	Nijmegen	The Netherlands
Maureen Junker-Kenny	Dublin	Ireland
Werner Jeanrond	Lund	Sweden
François Kabasele Lumbala	Mbuji Mayi	Zaire
Karl-Josef Kuschel	Tübingen	Germany
Nicholas Lash	Cambridge	Great Britain
Dietmar Mieth	Tübingen	Germany
John Panagnopoulos	Athens	Greece
Giuseppe Ruggieri	Catania	Italy
Elisabeth Schüssler Fiorenza	Cambridge, MA	USA
Christoph Theobald SJ	Paris	France
Miklós Tomka	Budapest	Hungary
David Tracy	Chicago, IL	USA
Marciano Vidal CSSR	Madrid	Spain
Felix Wilfred	Madras	India
Ellen van Wolde	Tilburg	The Netherlands

General Secretariat: Prins Bernardstraat 2, 6521 A B Nijmegen, The Netherlands
Manager: Mrs E. C. Duindam-Deckers

CONCILIUM

The Theological Journal of the 1990s

Now available from Orbis Books

Founded in 1965 and published five times a year, *Concilium* is a world-wide journal of theology. Its editors and essayists encompass a veritable 'who's who' of theological scholars. Not only the greatest names in Catholic theology, but also exciting new voices from every part of the world, have written for this unique journal.

Concilium exists to promote theological discussion in the spirit of Vatican II, out of which it was born. It is a catholic journal in the widest sense: rooted firmly in the Catholic heritage, open to other Christian traditions and the world's faiths. Each issue of *Concilium* focusses on a theme of crucial importance and the widest possible concern for our time. With contributions from Asia, Africa, North and South America and Europe, *Concilium* truly reflects the multiple facets of the world church.

Now available from Orbis Books, *Concilium* will continue to focus theological debate and to challenge scholars and students alike.

Please enter my subscription to **Concilium** 1998/1-5

[   ] individual US$60.00   [   ] institutional US$75.00

Please send the following back issues at US$15.00 each

1997 . . . . 1996 . . . .

1995 . . . . 1994 . . . .

1993 . . . . 1992 . . . .

[   ] MC/Visa . . . . . . / . . . . . . / . . . . . . / . . . . . Expires . . . .

[   ] Check (payable to Orbis Books)

Name/Institution . . . .

Address . . . .

City/State/Zip . . . .

Telephone . . . .

Send order and payment to:
Orbis Books, Box 302, Maryknoll, NY 10545-0302 USA

Concilium Subscription Information - outside North America

Individual Annual Subscription (five issues): £25.00

Institution Annual Subscription (five issues): £35.00

Airmail subscriptions: add £10.00

Individual issues: £8.95 each

New subscribers please return this form:
for a two-year subscription, double the appropriate rate

(for individuals)   £25.00   (1/2 years)   . . . .

(for institutions)   £35.00   (1/2 years)   . . . .

Airmail postage
outside Europe +£10.00   (1/2 years)   . . . .

Total . . . .

I wish to subscribe for one/two years as an individual/institution
(delete as appropriate)

Name/Institution . . . .

Address . . . .

. . . .

. . . .

I enclose a cheque for .... payable to SCM Press Ltd

Please charge my Access/Visa/Mastercard no. . . . .

Signature . . . . .Expiry Date . . . .

Please return this form to:
SCM PRESS LTD   9 - 17 St Albans Place   London   N1 0NX

GENERAL THEOLOGICAL SEMINARY
NEW YORK

DATE DUE

NOV 1			
APR 0 7 2003			
			Printed in USA

HIGHSMITH #45230